GLOBAL CHANGER

STUDENT'S BOOK AND WORKBOOK

2

MAURICIO SHIROMA, VERONICA TEODOROV,
LIZ WALTER AND KATE WOODFORD WITH PAULO MACHADO

CAMBRIDGE
UNIVERSITY PRESS

CONTENTS

* This material can be downloaded from the Digital Resource Pack.

WELCOME!

PLACES IN TOWN AND PREPOSITIONS OF PLACE

1 0.01 **Look at the map and complete the words for places in town. Listen, check, and repeat.**

1 g rocery s tore
2 b______ a______
3 c______ s______
4 p______
5 m______
6 m______ t______
7 r______
8 s______
9 s______

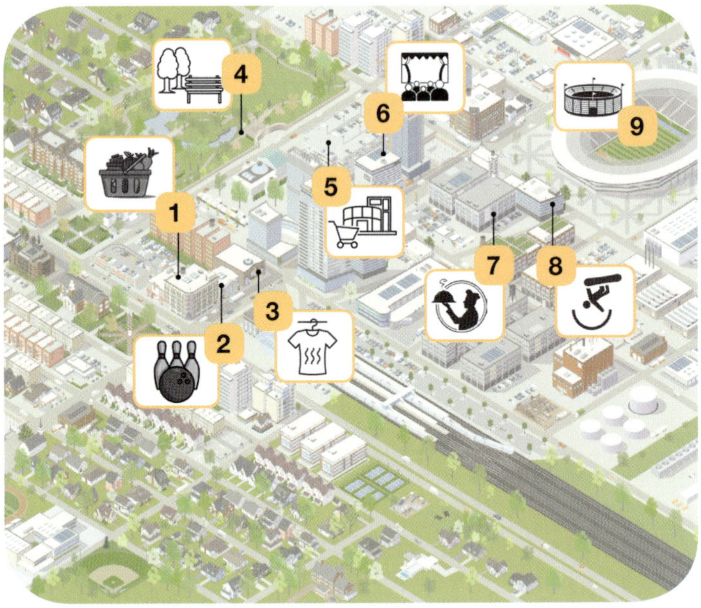

2 0.02 **Look at the map again and choose the correct options. Then listen to the dialogue and check.**

1 The skatepark is *behind* / *in front of* / *next to* the stadium.
2 The restaurant is *behind* / *in front of* / *next to* the skatepark.
3 The mall is *between* / *behind* / *in front of* the park.
4 The movie theater is *next to* / *inside* / *between* the mall.
5 The bowling alley is *inside* / *between* / *behind* the grocery store and the clothes store.
6 The grocery store is *on the left of* / *inside* / *on the right of* the bowling alley.

SUBJECT, OBJECT, AND POSSESSIVE PRONOUNS

LOOK!
Remember: never omit object pronouns.

3 **Complete the sentences with the correct subject, object, or possessive pronoun.**

1 His name is Mario.
2 I always want a drink after basketball, so my dad buys ______ a soda.
3 Victoria's mother called ______ on the phone, but she didn't answer.
4 Mark, this is not your pen. It's ______. Look, here's my name.
5 They have a new teacher. Mr. Suares teaches ______ English now.
6 You and I are tired. ______ need to rest.
7 I'm certain this is your bike. Yes, look, it's definitely ______!

ADVERBS OF FREQUENCY

1 Make questions with *how often* to ask a partner. Use the prompts.

1 go to the mall
How often do you go to the mall? ....
2 play soccer
....
3 read in bed
....
4 take the bus
....
5 have lunch at home
....
6 listen to music
....

FOOD

2 0.03 Complete the sentences with the words below. Then listen, check, and repeat.

- beans
- carrots
- cheese
- chicken
- fish
- orange juice
- pineapple
- ~~rice~~

a

Brazilian people love to eat [1] ....rice.... and [2] ....

b

Many Japanese people eat [3] .... and [4] .... in the same meal.

c

I made a delicious drink from [5] .... and [6] ....

d

I love the combination of [7] .... and [8] .... on a Hawaiian pizza.

TRANSPORTATION

3 0.04 Look and number the words. Then listen, check, and repeat.

1 motorcycle ....A....
2 airplane ....
3 subway ....
4 bus ....
5 boat ....
6 car ....

A

B

C

D

E

F

SIMPLE PAST OF VERB *TO BE*

1 Put the words in the correct order to make questions.

1 your / good / weekend / was / ?

Was your weekend good?

2 your / was / school / yesterday / at / best friend / ?

....

3 cafeteria / this morning / the / were / they / in / ?

....

4 and your family / at / on / were / Sunday / the beach / you / ?

....

....

5 year / teachers / the same / last / your / were / ?

....

SIMPLE PAST OF REGULAR AND IRREGULAR VERBS

2 Complete the review with the correct simple past form of the verbs in parentheses.

●●●●●

Great Location, Amazing Facilities

Bersantai is a beautiful hotel and it [1] didn't disappoint (not disappoint) me. I [2] .... (stay) there for two weeks in March. We [3] .... (eat) delicious food at the hotel restaurant. We [4] .... (not go) to the spa, but we [5] .... (relax) by the swimming pool. We [6] .... (walk) on the beach and we [7] .... (go) to the stores downtown. My brother [8] .... (take) cool photos at Mengiat Beach.

I [9] .... (not sleep) well on the first day because it was very hot. But then the weather [10] .... (change) and it was perfect.

[11] .... I .... (like) it? I [12] .... (love) it! We [13] .... (have) a great time there.

PERSONALITY ADJECTIVES AND FEELINGS

3 0.05 Circle the correct word to complete the sentences. Then listen, check, and repeat.

1

She's really **bored** / *boring* / *funny*.

2

She is *surprised* / *angry* / *strong*.

3

He was very *brave* / *friendly* / *tired*.

4

She's really *sad* / *excited* / *clever*!

5

Michael is so *amazing* / *happy* / *lazy*!

6

This is a *worried* / *kind* / *funny* picture.

NATURE

1 0.06 **Find ten nature words and label the images. Then listen, check, and repeat.**

F	H	I	L	L	N	C	G
V	I	F	L	O	W	E	R
I	U	E	E	B	B	L	A
L	S	A	L	Y	B	A	S
L	E	C	D	D	I	K	S
A	A	J	D	A	R	E	A
G	T	R	E	E	D	V	U
E	R	C	O	A	S	T	I

 1 field

 2 ....

 3 ....

 4 ....

 5 ....

 6 ....

 7 ....

 8 ....

 9 ....

 10 ....

PAST PROGRESSIVE

2 0.07 **Complete the sentences. Use the correct forms of the verbs below. Then listen and check.**

- look • not wear • show • sit • sleep • ~~watch~~ • wear

It was 10 o'clock last night. I [1] was watching some online videos. My parents [2] .... I got a message from my friend Sara. She [3] .... for her school jacket, but she couldn't find it. "I [4] .... my jacket at school today, right?" she asked me. "Yes, you were," I answered. "But you took it off in the classroom." She then asked, "I [5] .... next to Regina and Isabel, right?" "Yes, that's right," I replied. "At the end of the last class, you [6] .... them pictures on your cell phone and they [7] .... their jackets," I answered. "Maybe one of them took your jacket by mistake."

3 **Complete the questions with the correct past progressive form of the verbs below. Then match 1–5 with a–e.**

- drive • live • shout • talk • ~~watch~~

1 Were you watching TV last night? b
2 .... your mother .... to you? ....
3 .... we .... yesterday evening? ....
4 .... he .... to work at 9 a.m. today? ....
5 .... they .... in Spain in 2020? ....

a Yes, she was. She was telling me about her day.
b No, I wasn't. I was studying for a test.
c No, we weren't. We were just talking loudly.
d Yes, they were. They had an apartment in Madrid.
e Yes, he was. He missed the bus this morning.

THE WEATHER

1 0.08 **Look at the images and label the pictures with the weather words below. Then listen, check, and repeat.**

- cloudy
- foggy
- rainy
- ~~stormy~~
- sunny
- windy

1 

stormy

2 

____

3 

____

4 

____

5 

____

6 

____

PAST PROGRESSIVE AND SIMPLE PAST

2 **Complete the chart. Use the correct forms of the verbs below.**

- arrive
- call
- wait
- watch

Past Progressive and Simple Past	
when	We [1] ____________ a movie **when** the pizza [2] ____________.
while	Michael [3] ____________ me **while** I [4] ____________ for him at the station.

3 0.09 **Complete the sentences. Use the correct forms of the verbs in parentheses. Then listen and check.**

1 He was texting his friend **when** his phone died. (text/die)
2 He ____________ his bike **when** he ____________. (ride/fall)
3 She ____________ with her cake **when** she ____________ it. (walk/drop)
4 Their car ____________ down **while** they ____________ home. (break/drive)
5 She ____________ her homework **while** her cat ____________. (do/play)
6 I ____________ an email **while** my brother ____________. (send/draw)

1 LIVE IT UP!

UNIT GOALS

- Talk about festivals and celebrations.
- Read about some festivals around the world.
- Listen to a dialogue about a festival.
- Learn about the *Las Fallas* festival.
- Make and accept suggestions.

THINK!

1 **Look at the photo. What do you think the people are celebrating?**

2 **What kind of things do people celebrate?**

VIDEO 1.1

1 **What special things do festivals celebrate? Name three.**

2 **Where do people celebrate *La Guelaguetza*?**

VOCABULARY IN CONTEXT

LONG AND SHORT ADJECTIVES 1

1 Read the tweet. Then match the words in bold with their opposites 1–5 and label the images.

Maxine Taylor
@taylormax111

follow

At a Festival

I'm at the Holi Festival. I love it! It's very **lively**. People celebrate with colored powder and some **unusual** food. The streets are **crowded** with people. It's a lot of fun and very **noisy**! It brings color to a **dull** day! Do you know any similar festivals?

reply / send / favorite / more

Jan 5 ♡31

1

~~calm~~

lively

2

~~empty~~

3

~~exciting~~

4

~~quiet~~

5

~~traditional~~

2 1.01 Listen, check, and repeat.

3 **Look at the images and complete the sentences with the words below.**

- ~~calm~~
- crowded
- dull
- empty
- exciting
- lively
- noisy
- quiet
- traditional
- unusual

1

It feels very ____calm____ in our neighborhood when the street is ____________ of traffic and people.

2

It's really ____________ here! I can't hear you! Your voice sounds very ____________ – you need to shout!

3

The food at the festival was strange – it was very ____________. It was really ____________ to try a lot of new dishes.

4

The review said, "The movie is full of ____________ music," but it was so ____________ we left before the end.

5

The square wasn't ____________, so we could enjoy the ____________ dances and colorful costumes.

4 **Complete the chart with the words from Exercise 3. Then compare your answers with a partner.**

Positive Idea	Neutral Idea	Negative Idea
calm		

USE IT!

5 **Work in pairs. Take turns asking what your partner thinks about a festival or celebration in your country and answer using the words in Exercise 3.**

What do you think about the Rio de Janeiro Carnival?

I think it's exciting! It's …

READING

1 **Look at the images and posts. Check (✓) the correct answers.**

1 Which of these activities does Liz write about?
- ◯ travel to different countries
- ◯ be in silence
- ◯ go to an amusement park
- ◯ watch wild animals

2 Who is Liz?
- ◯ a scientist studying marine animals
- ◯ a student enjoying her vacation
- ◯ a person promoting a competition

LIZ TRAVELS,
in New York, USA

Remember my trips to South Africa and Indonesia earlier this year? This is your chance to win a free trip for two to one of these countries! Just follow me at @liztravels, post a photo, and include the hashtag #pickmeLizTravels (competition ends December 20). Good luck!

♡ liked by Jenna Martin and 12,579 others.
There are 45 comments in total.

LIZ TRAVELS,
in Hermanus, ZA

Guess where this is? South Africa! I went to the annual Hermanus Whale Festival, a three-day festival dedicated to a special type of whale: the southern right whale! How big or small are they? Well, this species is bigger than humpback whales and smaller than blue whales. You can go on a boat to get close to the whales. This is called whale watching. I learned so much about why we need to protect whales. Did you know that whales can live to be 100 years old?

♡ liked by Cory Stanton and 6,167 others.
There are 34 comments in total.

LIZ TRAVELS,
in Bali, ID

I took this photo while I was in Bali, Indonesia, in total silence. People there celebrate the New Year for six days in March or April. New Year in Indonesia is later than New Year in the USA. Day three of the celebrations is called Nyepi (the Day of Silence) and there's no electricity, no traffic, no work, and no school for 24 hours. It's a day of purification. Being quiet isn't easy, but it's easier than you think! After several hours, I felt calmer than I was before. And I loved it!

♡ liked by Taylor Smith and 4,621 others.
There are 20 comments in total.

2 1.02 **Read and listen to the posts. Which festival do the sentences describe? Write *H* (Hermanus Whale Festival), *N* (Nyepi), or *B* (both).**

1 People celebrate it in March or April. N
2 This is a festival that happens every year. ______
3 You can see animals in their natural habitat. ______
4 It's a quiet celebration. ______
5 The celebration is one day. ______

3 **Read the posts again and answer the questions.**

1 What do you have to post to enter Liz's competition?
a photo
2 Which species of whale do people see at the Hermanus Whale Festival?
______
3 Do people celebrate Nyepi at the beginning of their New Year celebrations?
______
4 Can people take the bus during Nyepi?
______

THINK!
What's your favorite celebration? Why? Do you want to travel like Liz? Why / Why not?

WORKBOOK p.115

LANGUAGE IN CONTEXT

1 **Look at the examples and the LOOK! box below. Complete the sentences from the posts on page 12.**

Comparatives: Short Adjectives

It's [1] bigger than the humpback whale.

They're [2] .... **than** blue whales.

New Year in Indonesia is [3] .... **than** New Year in New York.

Total silence isn't easy, but it's [4] .... you think!

2 **Circle the correct options.**

1 A car is *big* / *bigger* than a bike.
2 A bike is *cheap* / *cheaper* than a car.
3 My mom's food is *good* / *better* than restaurant food.
4 My grandpa is *old* / *older* than my grandma.
5 My cousin's dog is *quiet* / *quieter* than mine.
6 You look *happy* / *happier* than your friend today.

LOOK!

Irregular Comparatives	Regular Comparatives
bad – worse	small – smaller
good – better	late – later
far – farther	big – bigger

3 **Look at the adjectives for each festival. Match the opposite adjectives and write sentences to compare the two festivals.**

Carnival – Venice, Italy

1 big d
2 lively ....
3 long ....
4 new ....
5 noisy ....

Aoi Festival – Kyoto, Japan

a calm
b old
c quiet
d small
e short

1 The Venice Carnival is bigger than the Aoi Festival.
The Aoi Festival is smaller than the Venice Carnival.

2 ....
....

3 ....
....

4 ....
....

5 ....
....

USE IT!

4 **Compare two famous festivals in your country with a partner.**

The Rio de Janeiro Carnival is older than the Parintins Folklore Festival.

Yes, and it's ...

WORKBOOK p.112 and p.114 PRACTICE EXTRA

LISTENING AND VOCABULARY

FESTIVALS AND CELEBRATIONS

1 1.03 **Label the images with the words below. Then listen, check, and repeat.**

• ~~atmosphere~~ • crowds • dance show • fireworks • music event • souvenirs

1 

atmosphere

2 

....

3 

....

4 

....

5 

....

6 

....

2 **Look at the image and answer the questions.**

1 What type of festival do you think it is?

....

2 Which events from Exercise 1 do you think you can see there?

....

3 1.04 **Listen to Grace's description of the festival. Check your answers to Exercise 2.**

4 1.04 **Listen again and answer the questions.**

1 Where was Ryan during the Albuquerque Balloon Festival?

He was at his grandma's house in Florida.

2 Why did Grace go to the festival on a weekday this year?

....

3 How was the atmosphere at the event?

....

4 What did Grace and her parents buy to take home?

....

5 How much were the tickets to the festival this year?

....

6 Do the two friends want to go to the festival together next year?

....

WORKBOOK p.113

LANGUAGE IN CONTEXT

1 **Complete the sentences from the dialogue in the chart. Use the phrases below.**

- more modern than
- more tired than

Comparatives: Long Adjectives
The photos are **awesome**, but the real balloons are **more awesome than** the photos.
Last year's festival was **exciting**. This year's festival was **more exciting than** last year's!
I have a **modern** cell phone, but my new camera is [1] ______________ my cell phone.
My parents and I were **tired**. I was [2] ______________ my parents.

2 **Circle the option that is not possible in each sentence.**

1 The burgers were more *unusual* / *expensive* / *intelligent* than the hot dogs.

2 Modern dances can be more *difficult* / *nervous* / *interesting* than traditional dances.

3 The fireworks were more *exciting* / *organized* / *delicious* than the music events.

4 Last year's festival was more *recent* / *amazing* / *beautiful* than this year's celebration.

LOOK!

Comparatives: Long Adjectives

more + adjective + *than*

Soccer is **more exciting than** golf.

3 **Complete the sentences from the dialogue in the chart. Use the phrases below.**

- as colorful as
- as expensive as

Comparatives: (*not*) *as* ... *as*
The burgers were expensive. The pizzas were expensive, too.
The burgers were [1] ______________ the pizzas.
The photos are colorful. The real balloons are very colorful.
The photos aren't [2] ______________ the real balloons.

4 **Compare two places to eat. Complete the sentences with (*not*) *as* ... *as* and the adjectives in parentheses.**

1 Poncho Fries is n't as famous as Annie and Bennie's. (famous/not)

2 Annie and Bennie's is ______________ Poncho Fries. (big)

3 Annie and Bennie's is ______________ Poncho Fries. (old/not)

4 In terms of price, Poncho Fries is ______________ Annie and Bennie's. (expensive/not)

USE IT!

5 **Work in pairs. Rank these items 1–4 in order of their importance to you at a festival.**

- activities
- food
- location
- tradition

WORKBOOK p.112 and p.114 PRACTICE EXTRA

AROUND THE WORLD

1 **Look at the images and discuss the questions with a partner.**

1 What can you see?
2 What do you think is happening?

2 1.05 **Read and listen to the text. What is the text? Check (✓) the correct answer.**

◯ a narrative about a personal experience at a Spanish festival
◯ a description of an event in Valencia
◯ a report about an art festival that took place in March this year

3 **Check (✓) the correct option to complete the sentence.**

Nicky Schwartz …
◯ is an experienced and popular *fallero* from Valencia.
◯ gives opinions about some aspects of *Las Fallas.*
◯ writes about festivals all over the world.

This week in our series about festivals around the world:

LAS FALLAS FESTIVAL – VALENCIA

By Nicky Schwartz

LAS FALLAS (March 15 to 19)
is an awesome Spanish festival.

But what are *fallas*? Well, they're enormous structures with a specific theme, decorated with smaller sculptures called *ninots*. The *falleros*, or artisans from all over the city make the *fallas*. There are about 700 *fallas* every year, and each one takes a whole year to make! It's a traditional event, but you can find *ninots* of modern characters and celebrities, such as Shrek and … Lady Gaga! Yay! But there is a really unusual thing at *Las Fallas*. They burn everything at the end of the festival! Yikes! All that hard work! Well, at least they save one *ninot*. This lucky *ninot* goes to the Fallas Museum. Phew!

During *Las Fallas*, the streets are more crowded and noisier than the rest of the year because there are fireworks, live music, and food stalls – anyone love *paella*? Yummy! Don't miss the main event called *La Nit del Foc* (the Night of Fire), on March 18, with a spectacular fireworks show.

4 Read the text again. Match 1–5 with a–e.

1 dates of the festival ....a....
2 examples of *ninots* of a modern character and a celebrity ....
3 where the lucky *ninot* goes ....
4 time needed to make a *falla* ....
5 number of *fallas* in the festival ....

a March 15 to 19
b about 700
c one year
d Shrek and Lady Gaga
e the Fallas Museum

5 Read the sentences and write *T* (true) or *F* (false).

1 *Las Fallas* happen in Valencia every year. ....T....
2 This isn't the first article in a series. ....
3 The *fallas* are small sculptures. ....
4 *Falleros* are the people that make the *fallas*. ....
5 People destroy all the *ninots* in the end. ....

WORDS IN CONTEXT

6 Match 1–4 with a–d.

1 Phew! ....
2 Yay! ....
3 Yikes! ....
4 Yummy! ....

a

b

c

d

THINK!

Find out about a tradition that involves fire in your country.

WEBQUEST

Learn more! Check (✓) *True* or *False*.
The morning after *Las Fallas*, all the streets in Valencia are clean and quiet again.

○ **True** ○ **False**

VIDEO

1.2

1. **Name two festivals from around the world that have fireworks.**
2. **Which country probably invented fireworks?**

SPEAKING

MAKING AND ACCEPTING SUGGESTIONS

1 1.06 **Read and listen to Christine and Gabriella. What are they planning to do?**

Christine: Hey, Summerfest is next month. Why don't we go together?

Gabriella: Yeah, let's do that! I'd like to go to a rock concert. Where is it?

Christine: It's in the Apollo Club on George Street.

Gabriella: OK. Are the tickets expensive?

Christina: Ugh! It looks like we have to spend a lot of money. Do you want me to check for student discounts?

Gabriella: Yeah, that would be great! Oh, I can't wait to go!

LIVING ENGLISH

2 Read the dialogue in Exercise 1 again. Write the correct expressions.

Which expressions do they use to …

1 make a suggestion?

....

....

2 accept a suggestion?

....

....

3 1.07 **Listen, check, and repeat the expressions.**

PRONUNCIATION

4 1.08 **Listen and pay attention to the pronunciation of *have to* /'hæf tə/.**

/'hæf tə/

It looks like we **have to** spend a lot of money.

5 1.08 **Listen again and repeat.**

6 1.06 **Listen to the dialogue again. Then practice with a partner.**

7 Role play a new dialogue. Follow the steps.

1 Change the words in blue to write a new dialogue in your notebook.
2 Practice your dialogue with a partner.
3 Present your dialogue to the class.

YOUR DIGITAL PORTFOLIO

Record your dialogue. Then upload it to your class digital portfolio.

PRACTICE EXTRA

2

AMAZING PLACES

UNIT GOALS

- Talk about places and extreme weather.
- Read about different places in the world.
- Listen to an anecdote about an unusual trip.
- Learn about an amazing place.
- Write a travel blog.

THINK!

1 What's your favorite place to visit?

2 Imagine the perfect vacation. Where is it? Why is it perfect?

VIDEO 2.1

1 Name three countries from the video.

2 Name three examples of natural wonders.

VOCABULARY IN CONTEXT

LONG AND SHORT ADJECTIVES 2

1 2.01 **Complete Tim's posts with the words below. Then listen, check, and repeat the words.**

- amazing
- ~~awful~~
- busy
- cold
- dry
- hot
- incredible
- peaceful
- terrible
- wet
- wonderful

a **timtimaround** The weather is [1]a w f u l, really [2]_o___, but the view is awesome. 😍

b **timtimaround** I'm in the US now, looking at the Badlands. It's very [3]___y here and really [4]h___! I gotta go! 😎

c **timtimaround** This volcano is [5]_m_______! And it's still active … better go now. LOL

d **timtimaround** These hills create a [6]________f___ landscape. It's so [7]p_________ here, I'm relaxing just by looking at this view. ❤️

e **timtimaround** Nature IS [8]_n__________. A [9]_u___ beach, but not with people. It's full of umi-hotaru, or sea fireflies. 🤩

f **timtimaround** After some [10]t_________ hours of bad weather … Finally I'm deep in the sea in an underwater museum, [11]___t and happy! 😁

2 **Match posts a–f in Exercise 1 with images 1–6.**

1 timtimaround

c

2 timtimaround

3 timtimaround

4 timtimaround

5 timtimaround

6 timtimaround

3 **Look at the adjectives in the posts in Exercise 1 again and answer the questions.**

Which adjectives does Tim use to describe …

1 the weather? awful ______ ______ ______ ______

2 himself? ______

3 places and nature? ______ ______ ______ ______ ______

4 2.02 **How many syllables do the adjectives in Exercise 1 have? Which is the important syllable? Complete the chart and then listen and check.**

a ●	b ●•	c ●••	d •●•	e •●••
cold				

5 **Look at the images. Write two adjectives from Exercise 1 to describe the places.**

a lake

______
______

b cave

______
______

c beach

______
______

d desert

______
______

USE IT!

6 **Work in pairs. Describe the images in Exercise 5 to your partner. Do you agree?**

I think the lake is …

I agree, but I think it's also …

WORKBOOK p.117 PRACTICE EXTRA

READING

1 **Look at images a–c. Discuss what you can see with a partner.**

2 **Look at the images again and match them with places 1–3.**

1 The Nile River ....
2 Mount Everest ....
3 Angel Falls ....

EARTH HAS IT ALL

Are you planning to visit the longest river, the highest waterfall or the tallest mountain in the world? Check out this information about three amazing places!

The longest river on the planet is the Nile River. It goes through 11 countries in Africa. That's right ... 11! You can travel along the Nile: start by kayaking in Uganda and finish in busy Cairo with a visit to the famous pyramids.

You can't miss Angel Falls in Venezuela. It's the world's highest waterfall in Canaima National Park, a UNESCO World Heritage site. Fly over the jungle, see a lot of different animals, and go for a swim in the beautiful, clean water. Imagine all the stories you can tell about your trip to Venezuela.

What about climbing? Reaching the top of the tallest mountain in the world is an amazing but also terrifying experience. Mount Everest is located between Nepal and Tibet. Climbers can often experience everything, from the best sunny day to the worst rainy afternoon when climbing. But as the saying goes, no pain, no gain!

a

b

c

3 2.03 **Read and listen to the article. Then answer the questions. Write *N* (River Nile), *E* (Mount Everest), or *A* (Angel Falls).**

1 Which place is a UNESCO World Heritage site? ....A....
2 Which place is in more than two countries? ....
3 Which place is in only two countries? ....
4 Where can you see many different animals? ....
5 Where can it often be sunny and rainy on the same day? ....

4 **Read the sentences and write *T* (true) or *F* (false).**

1 It takes more than one day to travel by boat from the beginning to the end of the Nile. ....T....
2 It is very quiet on the whole Nile River. ....
3 Angel Falls is an important site for people around the world. ....
4 You can visit the world's highest waterfall by airplane. ....
5 Mount Everest is in Venezuela. ....

THINK!

What is marvelous about the places in the article?

WORKBOOK p.119

LANGUAGE IN CONTEXT

1 **Look at the examples below. Complete the sentences from the online article.**

Superlatives: Short Adjectives	
Regular	**Irregular**
Are you planning to visit [1] *the tallest* mountain? [2] ______ river is the Nile River. Angel Falls is [3] ______ world's ______ waterfall. That hotel has **the biggest** rooms.	Climbers can often experience from [4] ______ sunny day to [5] ______ rainy afternoon.

2 **Complete the sentences with the correct superlative form of the adjectives in parentheses.**

1 Death Valley, in California, is *the hottest* place on Earth. (hot)

2 Vatican City is ______ country in the world. (small)

3 The Pacific Ocean is ______ ocean in the world. (large)

4 ______ house in the world is located in Mumbai, India. (big)

5 People say Norway is ______ place to live. (good)

LOOK!

Irregular Superlatives	Regular Superlatives
bad – worst	small – smallest
good – best	large – largest
far – farthest	big – biggest

3 **Complete the sentences so they are true for you.**

1 ______ is the tallest student in my class.

2 ______ is my best friend.

3 ______ is the smallest object in my bedroom.

4 I think ______ is the worst movie!

USE IT!

4 **Work in pairs. Student A: cover the Student B column. Student B: cover the Student A column. Take turns reading your sentences to your partner. Your partner checks (✓) *True* or *False*.**

Student A	Student B
1 La Paz, in Bolivia, is **the highest** capital city in the world. (True)	1 ◯ True ◯ False
2 Brazil is **the** world's **largest** country. (False – it's Russia)	2 ◯ True ◯ False
3 ◯ True ◯ False	3 **The highest** mountains are in Asia. (True)
4 ◯ True ◯ False	4 Australia is **the** world's **largest** island. (False – it's Greenland)

WORKBOOK p.116 and p.118 PRACTICE EXTRA

LISTENING AND VOCABULARY

EXTREME WEATHER

1 **Look at the images. What do you think is the connection between Ken and the images?**

tsunami

forest fire

blizzard

hurricane

Ken

flood

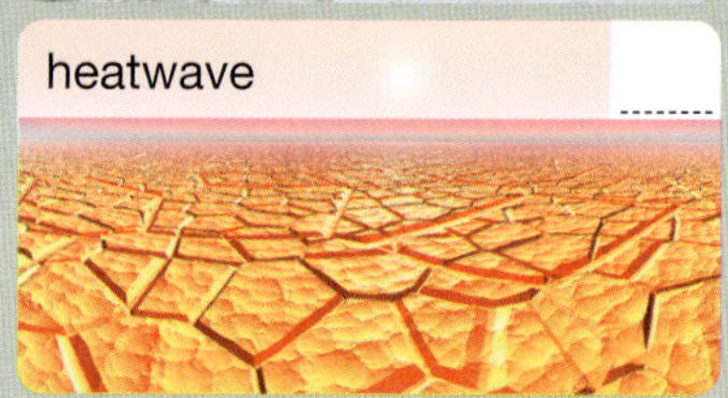
heatwave

thunderstorm

2 2.04 **Listen to Ken's story. Were your ideas in Exercise 1 correct? What's unusual about Ken's story?**

3 2.04 **Listen again and number the images in the order you hear them (1–7).**

4 2.05 **Listen, check, and repeat your answers to Exercise 3.**

5 **What do you think the weather is like in the images? Write the words and discuss your answers with a partner.**

1 cold ....
2 dry ....
3 hot ....
4 rainy ....
5 snowy ....
6 stormy ....
7 sunny ....
8 wet ....
9 windy ....

WORKBOOK p.117

LANGUAGE IN CONTEXT

1 Complete the sentences from Ken's story in the chart. Use the words/phrases below.

- beautiful
- most incredible
- the most difficult

Superlatives: Long Adjectives
Let me tell you about **the most impressive** experience I had.
I was in **the most** [1] ___beautiful___ hotel on a beach.
It was [2] __________ climb ever!
It was **the** [3] __________ dream.

LOOK!

That dream was **the most awful** experience!

Superlatives: Long Adjectives

the most + adjective

2 Write sentences with the prompts using the superlative.

1 People say Paris / beautiful / city in the world

People say Paris is the most beautiful city in the world.

2 That / unusual / festival in Europe

____

3 My city / hot / in the country

____

4 I think history / interesting / school subject

____

5 My room / peaceful / place in the house

____

6 This storm / bad / in years

____

3 Complete the sentences with a superlative and more information if necessary so they are true for you.

1 In my opinion, Rio de Janeiro is ___the most interesting___ city in the world.

2 The festival of __________ is __________ celebration in my community.

3 I think __________ is __________ app for teens.

4 My family is __________ thing to me.

5 My trip to __________ was __________ experience last year.

USE IT!

My sister is the most important person in my life.

4 Complete the chart with information about you. Then take turns sharing your information with a partner.

1 important person in your life	
2 beautiful place in the world	
3 interesting TV program	
4 good friend	
5 cold place in my country	

5 Write five sentences about your partner in your notebook.

WORKBOOK p.116 and p.118 PRACTICE EXTRA

WHITE SAND BEACH? NOT THIS ONE!

Posted by Julie Lewis, Jan 29

Hawaii is famous for the most beautiful beaches in the world, right? But imagine a beach with black sand! Welcome to Punalu'u beach, the most incredible beach in Hawaii, 48 kilometers from Hawaii Volcanoes National Park. Why is the sand black? Well, hot lava from the volcanoes went into the sea, immediately became solid, and eventually broke into very small pieces to make the sand.

The sun makes the black sand hot and this makes the beach the perfect place for turtles to make their nests. So be careful! Green sea turtles and even the endangered hawksbill turtles sit in the sun on the sand.

Tourists get excited about the black sand and some try to take it home as a souvenir. Please don't! The sand is very special. It's finite because it's old lava. The white sand beaches of Hawaii continue to have sand because fish bring sand to them, but not at Punalu'u. And we don't want Pele, the protector of volcanoes, to get mad at us!

Enjoy nature as it is and take home some good memories and amazing photos.

A sea turtle on Punalu'u beach

1 **What do you think makes a perfect beach? Make a list.**

2 **Look at the images and the text. Then discuss the questions with your partner.**

1 Do you think Punalu'u is a perfect beach? Why / Why not?
2 Why do you think Punalu'u beach attracts tourists?

3 2.06 **Read and listen to the text. Then correct the information in sentences 1–6.**

1 Punalu'u is in Hawaii Volcanoes National Park.
Punalu'u is 48 kilometers from Hawaii Volcanoes National Park.
2 Fish made the black sand.
....
3 The lava continued to be liquid in the sea.
....
4 The turtles make their nests in the sea.
....
5 The writer wants tourists to take home some black sand.
....
6 Pele is the protector of the beaches.
....

WORDS IN CONTEXT

4 **Match the words with their meanings.**

1	broke	a	animals or plants that may soon not exist
2	endangered	b	structure where animals lay their eggs and sometimes live
3	finite	c	that has an end
4	nest	d	separated suddenly into two or more pieces

5 **Read the text again. Number the events in order 1–5.**

a .... The lava went into the sea.
b .... The very small pieces of lava made black sand.
c .... The lava broke into very small pieces.
d ...1... The volcanoes made lava.
e .... The lava became solid.

THINK!

Why is it not OK to take home objects you find in nature as souvenirs?

WEBQUEST

Learn more! Check (✓) *True* or *False*.
There's a green sand beach in Hawaii.

○ **True** ○ **False**

VIDEO

2.2

1 **Which five countries have the most extreme places?**
2 **Why are these places special?**

WRITING

LOOKING FOR A DIFFERENT DESTINATION?
WHY NOT TRY **Patagonia?**

Why visit?

Patagonia in Argentina is one of the most beautiful places in the world!

What to see?

The incredible glacier, the Perito Moreno. One of the only glaciers in the world that is still growing! And don't forget to visit the village of El Chaltén and go hiking there.

When to go?

In the summer, from November to early March. The average temperature in the summer is 12°C. Temperatures are lower in the mountains, but the sun can be strong.

What to bring?

A windbreaker, a pair of gloves, a winter hat, a sun hat, and hiking pants (water-resistant are the best). Light items, always!

THE PERITO MORENO GLACIER

HIKING NEAR EL CHALTÉN

1 **Look at the blog. Check (✓) what it's about.**

- ◯ a story about Patagonia
- ◯ a travel agency
- ◯ recommendations for a trip

2 2.07 **Read and listen to the blog. Answer the questions.**

1 Where is Patagonia?

---

2 What places does the blog recommend?

---

3 When is summer in Patagonia?

---

4 Are the people in the images wearing the right clothes?

---

3 **Write a travel blog.**

1 Choose a place to write about.
2 Collect information about the place.
3 Find or draw images to illustrate the blog.
4 Write the first version of your blog. Use vocabulary from Unit 2.

4 **Switch your blog with a classmate and check their work. Use the checklist below.**

- ◯ title, questions, images
- ◯ labels for the images
- ◯ short sentences
- ◯ superlatives

LOOK!

Include questions to catch the reader's attention and organize your text in short sentences.

YOUR DIGITAL PORTFOLIO

Edit your blog. Then publish it. Upload it to the class portfolio for everyone to see!

REVIEW
UNITS 1 AND 2

VOCABULARY

1 Complete the sentences about five different festivals. Use the adjectives below.

• calm • ~~crowded~~ • dull • lively • unusual

1 I went to the festival, but it was very ___crowded___ and it was impossible to get good photos.
2 The festival in Ireland was ____________. It was a perfect place to rest and relax.
3 We loved the music and the ____________ atmosphere of the festival.
4 They invite monkeys to eat fruit and vegetables at this festival! It's really ____________!
5 The festival was really boring. The activities were ____________ and not interesting.

2 Look at the images and circle the correct options in sentences 1–4.

1 During our last vacation we could see the *atmosphere* / *fireworks* at night.

2 When I travel, I like to buy *fireworks* / *souvenirs* for friends and family.

3 I saw a traditional Korean *music event* / *dance show* at the Asian Center last Saturday.

4 This is a very popular festival and there are *crowds* / *fireworks* on the streets.

3 Complete the messages with the words below.

• awful • busy • peaceful • ~~terrible~~ • wet

Hey Cassia! Did you go to Coney Island on the weekend?

Yes, we did, but the weather was [1]___terrible___ on Saturday and we stayed in the hotel the whole day.

Oh, how [2]____________! Was the weather bad on Sunday, too?

No, it wasn't. We went to Deno's Wonder Wheel Park and everything was [3]____________ after the rain. But I was happy because the park wasn't [4]____________. On a normal day, there are a lot of people.

Good. Well, my weekend was [5]____________, very quiet. I read a book and ordered pizza!

4 Circle the odd one out.

1 thunderstorm / (dry) / hurricane
2 blizzard / heatwave / forest fire
3 tsunami / flood / heatwave
4 forest fire / blizzard / cold
5 hot / forest fire / thunderstorm
6 hurricane / wet / heatwave

LANGUAGE IN CONTEXT

5 Match 1–8 with a–h.

1 In my opinion, the NY Film Festival is ..e..
2 At the Music Fair, I learned that playing the guitar is ....
3 The Dongzhi Festival is in the winter when nights ....
4 The food at this year's rock festival ....
5 The Rock Music Fest is more ....
6 Tickets to the pop concert are ....
7 The ninots at the *Las Fallas* festival were ....
8 A hip-hop dance is ....

a easier than playing the piano.
b traditional than the NY Film Festival.
c was better than last year.
d more expensive than tickets to the opera.
e more organized than the Atlanta Film Festival.
f more exciting than watching a movie.
g are longer than days.
h bigger than our house!

6 Complete the sentences with the superlative form of the adjectives in parentheses.

1 The Venice Film Festival is ..the oldest.. (old) film festival in the world.
2 Oktoberfest is .... (large) German festival.
3 The Enrei Onodachi Memorial Festival is .... (short) festival in Japan.
4 In my opinion, *La Tomatina* is .... (happy) Spanish food festival.
5 Many people think that the Fuji Rock Festival is .... (clean) festival in the world.

7 Complete the dialogue with the superlative form of the adjectives below.

• amazing • ~~beautiful~~ • difficult • important

Hiro There's a very special beach on Iriomote Island, in Japan. I think it's [1] ..the most beautiful.. beach in the world. It's the Hoshizuna no Hama, or Star Sand Beach. The sand on this beach has the form of a star! It's [2] .... thing. But there's a problem. Some people collect sand and take it home with them.

Pam Oh, no. Convincing people to preserve the beach is probably [3] .... thing to do.

Hiro Yes, it is very difficult. For us, [4] .... thing now is the preservation of the beach. We want future generations to see this wonderful place.

LEARN TO LEARN

Reviewing Words

Review words at regular intervals (the following day, in a week, in a month, etc.) to help you memorize them.

CHECK YOUR PROGRESS

I CAN ...

- **talk about festivals and celebrations.**
- **use comparatives and (*not*) *as* ... *as*.**
- **talk about places and extreme weather.**
- **use superlatives.**

3 THE ART OF EMOTIONS

UNIT GOALS

- Talk about personality and art.
- Read about a special artist.
- Listen to a dialogue about art.
- Learn about the importance of art.
- Talk about a teacher.

THINK!

1 Describe this painting.
2 How do you feel when you look at this painting?

VIDEO 3.1

1 What colors are in the video?
2 What colors do we often see in hospitals?

VOCABULARY IN CONTEXT

PERSONALITY ADJECTIVES

1 3.01 **Read the article and try to complete the sentences with the personality words below. Then listen and check.**

- anxious
- cheerful
- creative
- easygoing
- independent
- mad
- negative
- patient
- ~~serious~~
- sociable

What does your favorite color tell you about your personality?

Black

You enjoy arts and music, and people say you are 1 serious. Sometimes you can be sad and 2 ________ about things.

Yellow

Like the sun, this is the color of warm and happy people. You have unusual ideas and people describe you as 3 ________.

Blue

Family and friends are very important to you. You are 4 ________ with other people and are always happy to wait your turn.

Pink

You are a 5 ________ person and like to be with other people. People see you as a romantic and sometimes innocent person.

Red

You are good with people and enjoy being the center of attention. But when people disappoint you, you can get 6 ________.

Gray

You always like to be in control of your emotions and you really don't want to feel 7 ________ or nervous.

Green

The natural world is important to you. You like to feel relaxed and people see you as a very 8 ________ person.

Orange

You are a very positive person. Things can be difficult, but you are always 9 ________. You want everybody to love you.

Purple

You like to have your own ideas and make your own decisions. People think you are a very 10 ________ person.

2 3.02 **Look at the images and complete the sentences with the words from Exercise 1. Then listen, check, and repeat the words.**

My name's Daniel. I think the two most important things about me are that I'm very [1] independent and [2] ________. I'm not sure my grandpa agrees! My grandpa can be very [3] ________ when we talk together, but he's never [4] ________. He's always positive.

I love to watch my grandma at work. She's really [5] ________ and takes a long time to make each item. She's very [6] ________.

All my sister's friends think she is very [7] ________, but I know she often feels [8] ________ before she goes out.

My little cousin is normally very [9] ________, but he gets [10] ________ when people say no to him.

3 **Check (✓) a color that you associate with each adjective in the chart.**

	black	blue	gray	pink	red	yellow	green	orange	purple
anxious	○	○	○	○	○	○	○	○	○
easygoing	○	○	○	○	○	○	○	○	○
cheerful	○	○	○	○	○	○	○	○	○
creative	○	○	○	○	○	○	○	○	○
independent	○	○	○	○	○	○	○	○	○
mad	○	○	○	○	○	○	○	○	○
negative	○	○	○	○	○	○	○	○	○
patient	○	○	○	○	○	○	○	○	○
serious	○	○	○	○	○	○	○	○	○
sociable	○	○	○	○	○	○	○	○	○

USE IT!

4 **Take turns choosing an image and tell a different partner how you feel about the colors.**

For me, gray makes me feel anxious.

Not for me. I think gray is a serious color.

WORKBOOK p.121 PRACTICE EXTRA

READING

1 **Check (✓) the sentences that are true for you and write one more way that you like to express yourself. Then discuss your ideas with a partner.**

- ◯ I like to draw, paint, and create things. Art expresses my feelings and emotions.
- ◯ I express myself best when I speak to people.
- ◯ I like to dance, move, and play sports. These are forms of expression, too.
- ◯ I ....

Autistic and Artistic: **The Story of Niam**

By Christine Baker

His paintings are full of energy and emotion.

Niam Jain is a typical teenager. He loves video games, pizza, and music. But he is also a quiet and creative artist with autism. He began painting at 12. Painting is important to him. He can express his ideas and feelings through art.

Speaking is very difficult for Niam. Some people with autism think in pictures, not in words, and Niam uses visual arts to communicate what's on his mind.

"I always know how he's feeling by what he paints. When he is mad, he uses a lot of red, for example," says Nina Jain, his mother. "Niam loves painting. It makes him cheerful and sociable."

Niam sells his paintings online and in galleries. His family was very surprised when he made $60,000 with his paintings! And that was just in one year!

"Working helps Niam," explains his mother. "I'm glad he's making money and he's becoming more independent. Niam has a passion and now he's making a career for himself." In the future, Niam and his family plan to open an art gallery not just for him, but for many other special artists.

Niam uses his art to say what he thinks.

2 3.03 **Read and listen to the article. Then complete the sentences with *W* (the writer) or *M* (Niam's mother).**

1 ...W... says that speaking is very difficult for Niam.
2 .... says some autistic people think in pictures.
3 .... thinks colors and feelings are connected.
4 .... says Niam made a lot money in one year selling his pantings.
5 .... believes working has benefits for Niam.

3 **Read the article again. Write *F* (fact) or *O* (opinion).**

1 His paintings are full of energy and emotion. ....
2 Painting makes Niam cheerful and sociable. ....
3 Niam is a teenage boy with autism. ....
4 It's difficult for Niam to communicate with words. ....

THINK!

What other activities can help autistic children?

WORKBOOK p.123

LANGUAGE IN CONTEXT

1 **Look at the examples and the LOOK! box below. Complete the sentences from the article.**

Gerunds	
Gerunds Before Verbs	**Gerunds After Verbs**
1 ___Painting___ is important to him.	Niam began 4 __________ at 12.
2 __________ is very difficult for Niam.	Niam loves 5 __________.
3 __________ helps Niam.	He likes 6 __________ his paintings online.

2 **Circle the correct options.**

1 *Taking* / *Making* photos is an art form, in my opinion.
2 My sister likes *running* / *singing* in her music class.
3 I don't like *studying* / *playing* very much, but I get good grades.
4 *Dancing* / *Painting* can be difficult, but I love colors.
5 I love *teaching* / *spending* my art to other people.

LOOK!

Gerunds

Use the *-ing* form of the verb to make a gerund.
read – reading
Reading is fun and interesting.

3 **Look at the images and complete the sentences. Use the gerund form of the verbs in parentheses.**

1

She likes ___watching___ her favorite movies in bed. (watch)

2

__________ poetry in English is very difficult for me. (read)

3

I like __________ because it's fun. (dance)

4
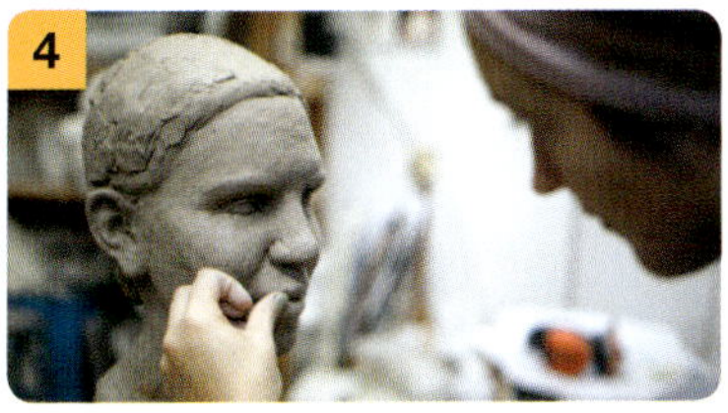
__________ is an incredible art. (sculpt)

5

__________ makes me feel very creative. (paint)

6

__________ isn't easy, but I'm taking classes. (act)

USE IT!

4 **Complete the sentences with gerunds so they are true for you. Then take turns sharing your sentences with a partner.**

1 __________ is fun and exciting. But I don't like __________.
2 __________ is relaxing.
3 I don't like __________. I think it's boring.
4 I like __________ when I'm tired.
5 __________ is __________.

Dancing is fun and exciting. But I don't like singing.

WORKBOOK p.120 and p.122 PRACTICE EXTRA

LISTENING AND VOCABULARY

ART

1 **What can you do with water and flour? Discuss your ideas with a partner and make a list.**

2 3.04 **Complete the advertisement with the words below. Then listen, check, and repeat the words.**

- ~~artist~~
- collages
- drawing
- graffiti
- mural
- stencils
- stickers
- technique

AFTER-SCHOOL ART PROGRAM

September 15 to November 15

Mondays and Fridays 2:30 to 4:30 p.m.

This is your chance to become an 1 *artist*! Learn all about different types of street art and become an expert at each 2 ______:

3 ______

4 ______

5 ______

6 ______

7 ______

Collaborate with other students and make a 8 ______

Hurry! Space is limited. See Ms. Garcia.

3 **Look at the image. Which of the techniques in the advertisement do you think the artists used?**

4 3.05 **Listen to a dialogue about artists in Buenos Aires. Were your ideas in Exercise 3 correct?**

5 3.05 **Listen again and complete the sentences with one word.**

1 Buenos Aires is one of the *best* cities in the world to see street art.
2 BA Paste Up is a ______ of artists from Buenos Aires.
3 BA Paste Up's messages make people ______.
4 Paste up art uses an ______ technique.
5 You make a mixture of ______ and flour to put the images on the walls.

WORKBOOK p.121

LANGUAGE IN CONTEXT

1 **Complete the sentences from the dialogue in the chart. Use the words below.**

• careful • creative • seriously • slowly

Regular Adverbs of Manner	
Adjectives	**Adverbs**
You are **slow**.	If you walk [1] ______, you can notice some street art.
They are [2] ______.	They think **creatively**.
I'm not a **serious** artist.	I don't work [3] ______.
I'm very [4] ______.	I always work **carefully**.

2 **Complete the sentences with the correct adverbs of manner using the words in bold.**

LOOK!

Adverbs of Manner

Regular	**Irregular**
quick – quick**ly**	good – well
happy – happi**ly**	fast – fast
careful – careful**ly**	hard – hard

1

The children are very **noisy**. They play ___noisily___ all day.

2

You know I'm **anxious**. Every day, I wait ______ for the bus.

3

I'm **good** at sports. For example, I play basketball ______.

4

The test was **hard**, but I studied ______ and got a good grade.

5

That artist is a **kind** person. She ______ agreed to draw me.

3 **Complete the sentences so they are true for you.**

1 I ______ slowly.
2 I ______ fast.
3 I ______ well.
4 I ______ carefully.
5 I ______ seriously.

USE IT!

4 **Work in pairs. Take turns asking about your partner's answers.**

What do you do slowly?

I eat slowly.

WORKBOOK p.120 and p.122 PRACTICE EXTRA

AROUND THE WORLD

1 **Can you see public art in your town? Do you like it? Why / Why not?**

2 **Look at the title, the image, and the first sentence of the text. What is the writer's inspiration?**

MY INSPIRATION

Look at this giant painting. Isn't it beautiful? Well, that's my school! I study at Rivadávia Corrêa Municipal School in downtown Rio de Janeiro. The Municipal Secretary of Culture selected it for the Rio Big Walls project in 2017, and an artist named Luna Buschinelli patiently painted it for around 10 hours a day for 45 days. The graffiti is so big that many people believe it's the world's biggest wall painting by a female artist! This came as a big surprise to me! I read that graffiti artists are usually men. Why is that? I believe women can be amazing graffiti artists, too!

The name of the graffiti mural is *Contos* (*Tales* in Portuguese). It's about a mother and her children. She's illiterate, but she uses her imagination to create and tell stories. And they're so incredible and magical that her children believe her stories really are from a book. Because of this painting, I and many other students at our school now have our hearts set on reading and writing. Learning how to read and write changes your life forever.

Luna is my role model, and now that I can read and write, I'm drawing regularly, too, because one day I want to become a graffiti artist like her.

3 🔊 3.06 **Read and listen to the text. Number the events in order 1–5.**

a .... The Municipal Secretary of Culture selected Rivadávia Corrêa Municipal School.

b ....1..... The Municipal Secretary of Culture started the *Rio Big Walls* project.

c .... Many students in Rivadávia Corrêa Municipal School became interested in reading and writing.

d .... The author started drawing regularly to become a graffiti artist one day.

e .... Luna Buschinelli began painting the mural.

4 **Read the text again and check (✓) the correct sentences.**

- ◯ The Municipal Secretary of Culture is in downtown Rio de Janeiro.
- ◯ Luna Buschinelli took about 450 hours to paint the mural.
- ◯ The mother in the mural is inventing a story for her children.
- ◯ The mural is officially the world's biggest wall painting by a female artist.
- ◯ The author likes Luna's work so much that she wants to become a graffiti artist in the future.

WORDS IN CONTEXT

5 **Look at the words in bold. Then match 1–4 with a–d.**

1 Our science project won first prize. It **came as a big surprise to** us. ....

2 Eduardo **has his heart set on** traveling to Europe. ....

3 My grandpa is **illiterate**. ....

4 My aunt Luisa is my **role model**. ....

a She's a creative and patient teacher.

b We were very happy with the news.

c He's working very hard to make money.

d I read stories to him.

THINK!

Do you believe public art can influence people to study and learn? Why / Why not?

WEBQUEST

Learn more! Check (✓) *True* or *False*.
It's illegal to use street art, in any form, without permission from the artist in your country.

◯ **True** ◯ **False**

VIDEO

3.2

1 What is the oldest type of art?

2 What different types of art are in the video?

SPEAKING

ASKING FOR AND GIVING CLARIFICATION

1 3.07 **Read and listen to Raul and Debbie talking about a teacher. How does Debbie feel about her art teacher?**

Raul Who's your art teacher?

Debbie Ms. Gloria Sánchez. You know, the new teacher from Spain. She's the real deal!

Raul What do you mean by that?

Debbie She's the best teacher. We love hearing about color theory. And she gives us a lot of good tips.

Raul In other words, her class is fun.

Debbie Yes! You can say that again!

LIVING ENGLISH

2 **Read the dialogue in Exercise 1 again. Then complete the mini dialogues with the expressions below.**

- the real deal
- what do you mean by that
- you can say that again

1 A This new song is awesome.
B Well, ...!

2 A Ms. Sánchez is ....!
B I know. Her classes are a lot of fun.

3 A This math problem is a piece of cake.
B Oh, ...?
A It's very easy.

3 3.08 **Listen, check, and repeat the expressions.**

PRONUNCIATION

4 3.09 **Listen and pay attention to the pronunciation of *ea* /iː/.**

1 Who's your art t**ea**cher? 2 She's the r**ea**l d**ea**l! 3 We love h**ea**ring about color theory.

5 3.09 **Listen again and repeat.**

6 3.07 **Listen to the dialogue again. Then practice with a partner.**

7 **Role play a new dialogue. Follow the steps.**

1 Change the words in blue to write a new dialogue in your notebook.
2 Practice your dialogue with a partner.
3 Present your dialogue to the class.

YOUR DIGITAL PORTFOLIO

Record your dialogue. Then upload it to your class digital portfolio.

PRACTICE EXTRA

4

LIFESTYLES

UNIT GOALS

- Talk about money and shopping.
- Read about a different lifestyle.
- Listen to people talking about different shopping options.
- Learn about ways people help others.
- Write about a lifestyle.

THINK!

1 Do you think people in houseboats have good lives? Why / Why not?

2 What is the perfect lifestyle for you?

VIDEO

4.1

1 What is a vegan?

2 How can you produce your own food? Name two ways.

VOCABULARY IN CONTEXT

SHOPPING 1

1 Look at the quiz. Match the words in bold in questions 1–10 with images a–j and label the images.

Are you good with money?

1. Do you get **spending money**?
   ◯ Yes ◯ No
2. Do you **spend** all the money you have every week?
   ◯ Yes ◯ No
3. Do you **save** money to buy something you like?
   ◯ Yes ◯ No
4. Do your brothers and sisters **borrow** money from you?
   ◯ Yes ◯ No
5. Do you do any activity in your free time to **earn** money?
   ◯ Yes ◯ No
6. Do you keep **coins** in a special place?
   ◯ Yes ◯ No
7. Do you keep **bills** in your school bag?
   ◯ Yes ◯ No
8. Do you know how to use an **ATM**?
   ◯ Yes ◯ No
9. Do you have a **debit card**?
   ◯ Yes ◯ No
10. Can you live without **money** for a day?
    ◯ Yes ◯ No

Now check your answers!

MORE "YES" ANSWERS

You're a money expert. You're really good with your money! You know how to spend your money on good things and save some for the future. Keep up the good work!

MORE "NO" ANSWERS

You're a money learner. You need to learn a little more about money. Find new ways to save your money and plan how to use your money. You know you can do it!

a earn ....

b ....

c ....

d ....

e ....

f ....

g ....

h ....

i ....

j ....

2 4.01 Listen, check, and repeat.

3 **Take the quiz. Read the questions and check (✓) the correct answers for you.**

4 **Write the words below in the correct box in the diagram.**

- ~~ATM~~
- bills
- borrow
- coins
- debit card
- earn
- money
- save
- spend
- spending money

Nouns

ATM
....
....
....
....
....

Money

Verbs

....
....
....
....

5 **Complete the sentences with the nouns and the correct form of the verbs in Exercise 4.**

1 I keep all my small ....coins.... in a glass jar. I'm .... money because I want to buy a new T-shirt.

2 My sister .... $5 dollars for walking my uncle's dog. He always gives her five-dollar ....

3 I .... a lot of .... on pens because I often lose them.

4 My cousin always .... money from me on Saturdays. That's the day my parents give me my ....

5 When I go shopping I use my .... to get money from the .... in the mall.

USE IT!

6 **Read sentences 1–6 and circle the correct option for you. Then take turns saying your sentences to a partner.**

1 I *can / can't* save money.
2 I *always / sometimes / never* get spending money.
3 I *know / don't know* how to use an ATM.
4 I *earn / don't earn* money when I help at home.
5 I *like / don't like* to keep my coins in my wallet.
6 I *spend / don't spend* my money on clothes.

WORKBOOK p.125 PRACTICE EXTRA

READING

1 **Discuss the answer to the questions with a partner.**

1 Do you need all the material things you have?
2 Could you live without these things? Why / Why not?

LIVING WITH LESS

Carolina Silva – Brazil

I want to tell you about Jacquie, my friend in the US. She's a freegan. What's a freegan, you ask? Well, Jacquie looks for useful things in trash cans, but she isn't poor. Freegans are a combination of "free" and "vegan." They rescue things in good condition that people throw away like furniture, clothes, and, of course, food.

I liked the idea of freeganism. I found some information on the Internet and decided to try some ideas for a month.

- I needed a dress for our school prom. I posted a note on the donation board and got three offers! I didn't pay anything and I got a beautiful dress!
- My friend wanted an apple pie for her birthday party. It was late when I arrived at the street market. There weren't any apples. But a man was putting a box of lemons into his van. Two fell on the street and he gave them to me. I baked a delicious lemon pie for my friend!
- I went to free concerts and cultural activities, and I walked in the park. I didn't spend any money!

This last month made me think. Now, I look at the donation board. When I cook, I try to use all of the vegetables, including the skins. I'm reusing more of my stuff and spending more time outside. Freeganism is a great lifestyle! 🙂

2 4.02 **Read and listen to the blog. Then read the sentences and write *T* (true) or *F* (false).**

1 Jacquie and Carolina don't go to the same school. T
2 Freegans throw away a lot of food. ______
3 Carolina decided to try some ideas for six weeks. ______
4 She couldn't buy all the ingredients for her recipe. ______
5 She's now staying at home more. ______

3 **Read the blog again. Write the words for definitions 1–5.**

1 containers for things you don't want trash cans
2 tables, beds, closets, etc. ______
3 graduation party ______
4 exterior part of a carrot, for example ______
5 things you have ______

THINK!

Carolina says, "Freeganism is a great lifestyle!" Do you agree?

WORKBOOK p.127

LANGUAGE IN CONTEXT

1 **Look at the examples below. Complete the sentences from the blog.**

Nouns		
	Countable	**Uncountable**
Affirmative (+)	I decided to try **some** [1] ideas for a month. She wanted **an** [2] ________ ________.	I found **some** [5] ________ on the Internet. She drank **some orange juice**.
Negative (–)	There [3] ________ **any apples**.	I didn't spend [6] ________ **money**.
Questions (?)	What's **a** [4] ________, you ask? Do you have **any coins**?	Is there **any furniture** in your new apartment?

2 **Are words 1–8 countable or uncountable? Write *C* (countable) or *U* (uncountable).**

1 apple C
2 bike ______
3 bread ______
4 cheese ______
5 soda ______
6 spaghetti ______
7 student ______
8 sweater ______

LOOK!

Countable and Uncountable Nouns

You can count countable nouns: **one** apple, **two** apples, etc.

You can measure uncountable nouns: **a kilo of** sugar, **a liter of** water.

3 **Complete the dialogue with *a*, *an*, *some*, or *any*.**

Han Are you [1] a freegan?
Pam No, not really. I just want to save [2] ________ money.
Han Do you buy [3] ________ clothes?
Pam No, I don't buy [4] ________ clothes.
Han How do you do it? You always look great.
Pam I use the clothes my brother and sister aren't wearing anymore.
Han That's awesome.
Pam I reuse [5] ________ things, too. Accessories, furniture …
Han Right. That's [6] ________ incredible pair of jeans, by the way.

USE IT!

4 **Work in pairs. Imagine you want to be a freegan. Tell your partner five things you want to do. Use countable and uncountable nouns.**

I want to save some money every week.

I want to go to a street market.

LISTENING AND VOCABULARY

SHOPPING 2

1 **Look at the image and discuss with a partner. What's happening in the image? How does it make you feel?**

2 **4.03 Label images 1–8 with the words/phrases below. Then listen, check, and repeat.**

- afford
- ~~bargain~~
- customer
- donate
- free
- price
- sales associate
- shopping center

1 

bargain

2 

....

3 

....

4 

....

5 

....

6 

....

7 

....

8 

....

3 **4.04 Listen to Jake and Mandy talk about shopping. Which day do you think the image in Exercise 1 shows? Which other days do they talk about?**

4 **4.04 Listen again. Who says sentences 1–5? Write *J* (Jake) or *M* (Mandy).**

1 Many people spend a lot of money at shopping centers. J

2 Nothing is free on Black Friday. ....

3 When I want to buy something, I check the price. ....

4 If it's a bargain, I buy it. ....

5 People donate things and we volunteer as sales associates. ....

6 Then customers come and pay what they can afford. ....

5 **Mandy says, "Black Friday is only about excessive consumerism." Do you agree? Why / Why not?**

WORKBOOK p.125

LANGUAGE IN CONTEXT

1 **Complete the sentences from the dialogue in the chart. Use the words and the LOOK! box below.**

• a lot of • ~~many~~ • money • people • spend

Quantifiers		
Countable	**How** [1] ___many___ times did you buy without thinking last month? **How many** sweaters did you buy?	There are [3] ______ incredible things to look at! **Many** teenagers prefer to save their money. **Not many** [4] ______ need all those things.
Uncountable	**How much** [2] ______ do you spend on Black Friday? **How much** information is there about the new video game?	Many people [5] ______ **a lot of** money at shopping centers. There isn't **much** time to rest on weekends.

2 **Complete the questions with *much* or *many*.**

1 How ___many___ T-shirts do you have?
2 How ______ students are there in your class?
3 How ______ food is there in the fridge?
4 How ______ classes do you have at school today?
5 How ______ money do you save every week?

LOOK!

We use quantifiers: *a lot of*, *much*, and *many* to talk about quantity.

I have **a lot of** books on my desk.

3 **Circle the correct options.**

1 Ray has *much* / *a lot of* video games.
2 Sarah and Kate don't have *many* / *much* time to go to the swimming pool.
3 There are *many* / *much* customers in the grocery store today.
4 I want to donate *much* / *a lot of* books to the library.
5 Justine is helping her grandma, so she has *a lot of* / *much* things to do.

USE IT!

4 **Make questions with the prompts and interview a partner. Take turns asking and answering, and complete the chart. Compare your answers.**

	You	Your Partner
1 money / spend / on the weekend?		
2 movies / see / TV / last month?		
3 spending money / get / a month?		
4 coins / need / buy your favorite candy?		
5 online games / play / on Saturdays?		

How much money did you spend on the weekend?

I spent a lot of money! I spent …

WORKBOOK p.124 and p.126 PRACTICE EXTRA

ACROSS THE CURRICULUM

MATH

HAPPY TO HELP!

Top-trending volunteer work

1. Dog walker
2. Personal shopper for elderly people
3. Math tutor at the school club

How volunteer work increased over the years

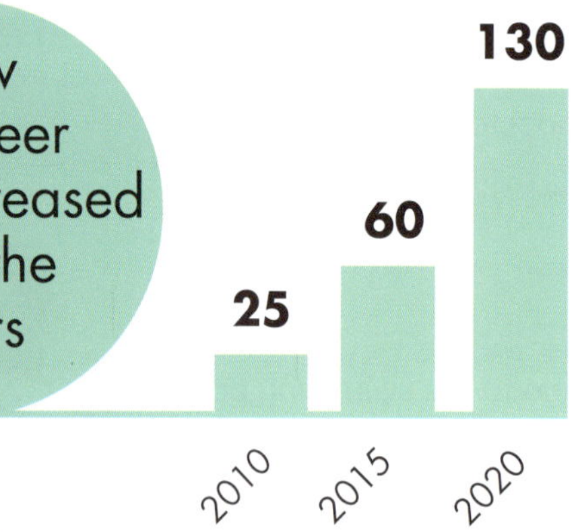

Time spent on volunteer work per week, except weekends

8 hours

The most popular types of volunteer work among teens age 12–14 in 2020

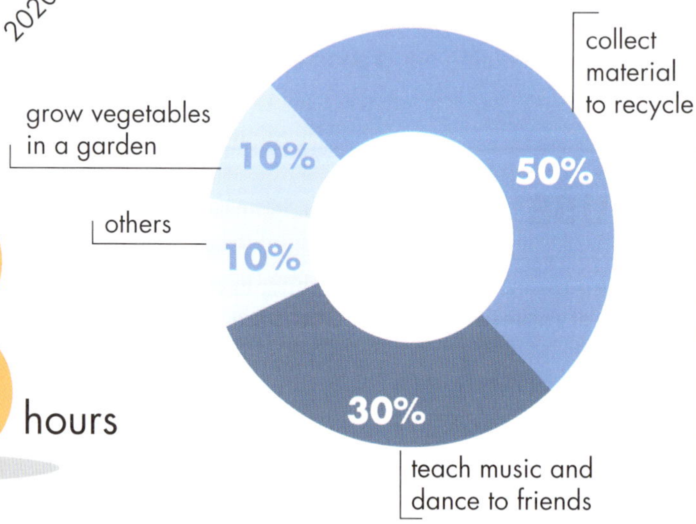

WHY are more teens using their time to help other people?

1st You get to meet nice people.

2nd You help people with something they really need.

3rd It shows you can make a difference. It feels great to help other people.

4th You give back to your community at the same time as learning new skills.

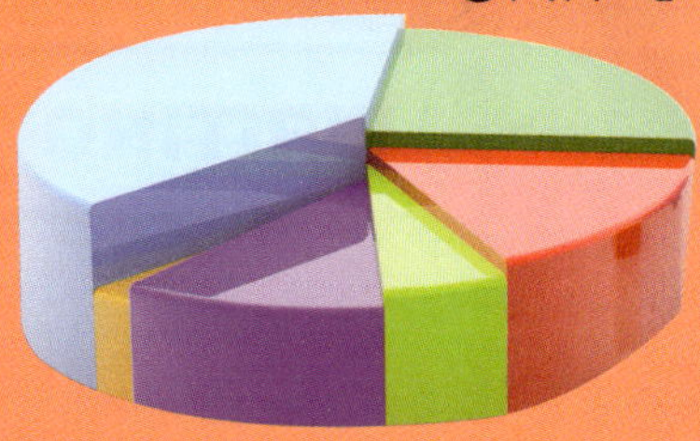

1 **Do you ever do volunteer work? Discuss the question with a partner.**

2 **Look at the infographic. What can you see? Check (✓) the correct option.**

- ◯ facts and figures about volunteer work
- ◯ opinions about volunteer work

3 4.05 **Read and listen to the text. Check (✓) the correct answers.**

1 How much did volunteer work increase between 2010 and 2015?
   a ◯ 40%   b ◯ 60%   c ◯ 140%

2 How many teenage students grew vegetables in a garden in 2020?
   a ◯ 13   b ◯ 65   c ◯ 39

3 How many hours a day does a teenager do volunteer work?
   a ◯ 1.6   b ◯ 2   c ◯ 1.3

4 4.05 **Read and listen again. Check (✓) the best conclusion for the infographic.**

- ◯ More teenagers are volunteering every year.
- ◯ Teenagers like science more than animals.
- ◯ You can't volunteer if you're a adult.

WORDS IN CONTEXT

5 **Complete the sentences with the words/phrases below.**

• dog walker • elderly • give back • make a difference

1 You can ________________ with your health. Eat good food and exercise!
2 I had a new job last summer. I was a ________________. I love animals.
3 My neighbor is an ________________ man from Spain. He's 95 years old!
4 Many students ________________ to the community by working as volunteers.

THINK!

How do you make a difference in other people's lives when you volunteer?

WEBQUEST

Learn more! Check (✓) ***True*** **or** ***False*****.**

PETA is an organization that helps people.

◯ **True**   ◯ **False**

VIDEO

4.2

1 **How many people volunteer each year?**
2 **Is it easy to find the perfect volunteer work for you? Why/Why not?**

WRITING

1 4.06 **Read and listen to the post. Check (✓) the correct answers.**

1 Who wrote the post?
- ◯ a student
- ◯ a teacher

2 Where can you read the post?
- ◯ on the school blog
- ◯ on Mr. Ling's blog

WHAT DO YOU KNOW ABOUT DIFFERENT LIFESTYLES?

We asked our teachers what they can remember from their childhood.

Mr. Ling, *math teacher*

1 My grandma was a very hardworking person. She had a beautiful garden and she always picked a lot of vegetables to cook. She was a vegetarian and when we spent our summer vacations with her, we didn't eat any meat.

2 The best part was when we helped her carry all those fresh vegetables in a basket. I loved the smell of the carrots, the lettuce, the green peas … and the tomatoes were delicious and very fresh, of course!

3 It was great to learn how to choose the best vegetables. Now, every time I go to the market, I know how to select the freshest and most delicious vegetables. I always buy the best.

2 **Read the post again. Match paragraphs 1–3 with a–c.**

a lesson learned ....   b introduction ....   c significant moment ....

3 **Study the examples in the LOOK! box. Then circle all the simple past verbs in the post. Underline another lesson learned in the simple present.**

4 **Write a post for the school blog.**

1 Choose a relative or friend with a different lifestyle to write about.
2 Think of a moment when you learned something positive about his/her lifestyle.
3 Find or draw an image to illustrate your post.
4 Write the first version of your post. Use vocabulary from Unit 4.

5 **Switch your post with a classmate and check his/her work. Use the checklist below.**

- ◯ title and image (your name and your photo)
- ◯ introduction
- ◯ significant moment using simple past verbs
- ◯ lesson learned using simple present verbs

LOOK!

Use the simple past and the simple present for specific purposes in your post. Look:

She **had** a beautiful garden and she always **picked** vegetables to cook. (a past experience)

Now, every time I **go** to the market, I **know** how to select the freshest and most delicious vegetables. (a lesson learned)

YOUR DIGITAL PORTFOLIO

Edit your post. Then publish it. Upload it to the class portfolio for everyone to see!

REVIEW
UNITS 3 AND 4

VOCABULARY

1 Circle the correct options.

1 Will is very *sociable* / *creative*. He has new ideas every day.
2 Nadia is a nice friend, always positive and happy. She's *independent* / *cheerful*.
3 Rick isn't OK. He's too *anxious* / *easygoing*. I think he's worried about something.
4 Dan and Tom aren't funny. I don't know why they're so *mad* / *serious*.
5 Celine is a good parent. She's calm and *patient* / *negative*.

2 Match 1–6 with a–f.

a

b

c

d

e

f

1 graffiti ..b..
2 drawing ....
3 collage ....
4 stickers ....
5 mural ....
6 artist ....

3 Match 1–5 with a–e.

1 I need to save my ..c..
2 She didn't have a $10 bill, ...
3 Fred is going to stop at ....
4 Ian earns good money ....
5 I want to use my spending money ....

a so she used her debit card.
b on the weekend at his dad's store.
c money and not spend it.
d to buy a snack at the cafeteria.
e the ATM to get some money.

4 Complete the messages with the words below.

• afford • bargain • free • shopping center

Let's go to the [1] ....
I don't have any money for the bus.
We can walk. It's [2] ....

I know. I need to keep all my money for a present for my mom.
We can check for a [3] ....
You're right. Maybe there's something I can [4] ....

LANGUAGE IN CONTEXT

5 **Put the letters in the correct order to write verbs. Then complete the sentences with the gerund form.**

1 ...watch... (wthac): ...Watching... series is what I like to do every evening.
2 .... (andec): .... is my sister's favorite weekend activity.
3 .... (tinpa): .... helps me express my feelings and emotions.
4 .... (ngsi): .... in my bedroom makes me happy.
5 .... (eadr): .... new books helps me learn more about art.

6 **Complete the sentences with the correct adverbs of manner using the adjectives in parentheses.**

1 Doris ...kindly... agreed to help with the mural. (kind)
2 He didn't come to school today. He doesn't feel .... (good)
3 Our neighbors left very .... this morning. I need to go to bed early tonight! (noisy)
4 They don't take her .... as an artist because she can't draw. (serious)
5 Can you speak ...., please? (slow)

7 **Look at the items in images 1–6. Write *C* (countable) or *U* (uncountable).**

1

U

2

......

3

......

4

......

5

......

6

......

8 **Complete the sentences with *much*, *many*, or *a lot of*.**

1 I don't have ...much... time. I have to go home now.
2 Art books are very expensive, so she doesn't have ....
3 .... students in my class don't have a debit card.
4 How .... money is in your wallet?
5 How .... apples do we need for lunch?

CHECK YOUR PROGRESS

I CAN...

- talk about personality and art.
- use gerunds and adverbs of manner.
- talk about money and shopping.
- use countable and uncountable nouns, and quantifiers.

LEARN TO LEARN

Word Charts

Write example sentences related to a word.

MONEY
- My sister has some bills and coins on her table.
- I don't get any spending money.
- I have a debit card.

5

LET'S TALK.

UNIT GOALS

- Talk about communication.
- Read about the future of communication.
- Listen to a dialogue about translating apps.
- Learn about sign languages around the world.
- Talk about what you want to buy.

THINK!

1 How many different ways can people communicate?

2 What do you think are good ways of communicating?

VIDEO

5.1

1 Where do emojis come from?

2 How do emojis help us communicate better?

VOCABULARY IN CONTEXT

COMMUNICATION 1

1 5.01 **Complete the quiz with the words below. Then listen, check, and repeat.**

- call
- ~~communicate~~
- emojis
- face-to-face
- language
- messages
- text
- video chat
- virtual communication

2 **Read and answer the questions in the quiz. Circle A, B, or C. Then check your results.**

COMMUNICATION!

How do you usually [1] communicate with your friends?

A.
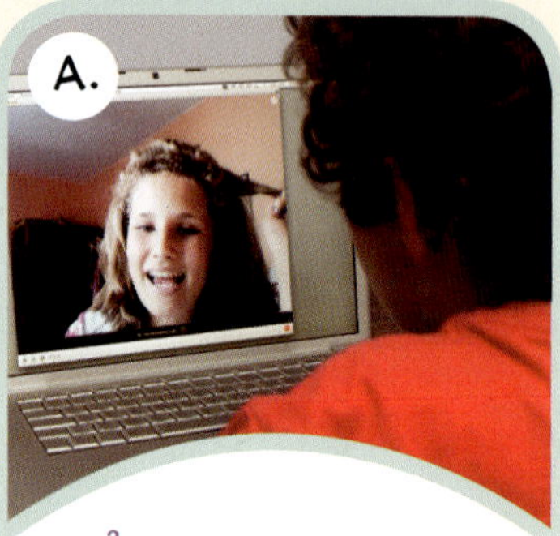
[2] ______

B.

I [3] ______ all the time!

C.

phone [4] ______ or email

How often do you have [5] ______ conversations with friends?

A. never B. sometimes C. always

Is your [7] ______ different in [8] ______?

A. Yes, I abbreviate words and don't use punctuation.

B. A little, because I use shorter sentences.

C. No, it's the same.

How often do you include [9] ______ in your messages?

A. always

B. sometimes

C. never

Which do you use more often?

A. phone messaging app

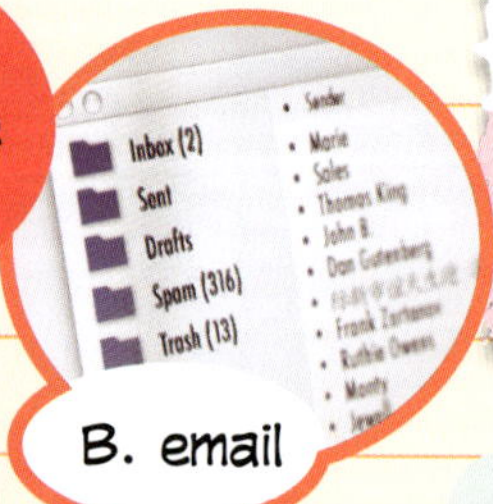

B. email

C. sticky note [6] ______

Do you talk to two or more people at the same time?

A. always B. sometimes C. never

◯ **TECHNOPHILE** ▶ More As – You love technology! You always have your phone in your hand. You're a modern communicator. Try to meet and talk to people in real life more often!

◯ **NOT TOO MUCH TECH** ▶ More Bs – You like your phone, but you don't use it too much, especially for texting. But you generally have the correct balance. Congratulations!

◯ **TECHNOPHOBE** ▶ More Cs – You use your phone to call your friends, so you know it's OK to use technology to communicate, right? Try it more often!

3 **Circle the correct options.**

1 My baby sister makes a lot of noise, but we can't understand her *emojis* / *language*
2 Some people don't *communicate* / *call* well when they use virtual communication.
3 Please don't *text* / *video chat* me the same message twice if I don't answer you immediately!
4 My dad gets up late, so I often leave him a *call* / *message* on the kitchen table.
5 I like *virtual* / *face-to-face* communication with my friends, so I can see them.

4 **Complete the chart with the words from Exercise 1.**

How We Communicate Ideas	Verbs Related to Communication	Nouns Related to Communication	Adjectives Related to Communication
[1] l______	call	[4] c______	[8] f______
	[2] c______	[5] e______	-t______
	[3] t______	[6] m______	-f______
		[7] v______	[9] v______
		c______	(communication)

5 **Complete the dialogue using all the words in the chart in Exercise 4.**

A I want to communicate with people around the world.
B Well, I'm learning a new language online.

______
______
______
______

USE IT!

6 **Answer the questions for you. Then work in pairs and discuss the questions.**

	Yes	No
1 Is it OK to call a friend after 11 p.m.?		
2 Do some people communicate better using texts?		
3 Do emojis help communication?		
4 Is a face-to-face conversation always better than virtual communication?		
5 Is it important to begin a message with "Hello" or "Good morning"?		
6 Do all people hate video chat because they don't want people watching them?		

I don't think it's OK to call a friend after 11 p.m.

I don't agree. I often call my best friend late at night.

WORKBOOK p.129 PRACTICE EXTRA

READING

1 **Do you read magazines? Why / Why not?**

2 **Do you think there is a difference between reading a magazine article and a blog post? Which do you prefer? Discuss your ideas with a partner.**

The Future of Communication

How will we communicate with each other in the future? Will it be very different? Here are some predictions about the future of communication.

Smartphones

We will have Bluetooth devices in our ears and eyes, and use implants in our hands to replace smartphones. Smartphones will be part of our bodies.

Telepathy

Sensors in our heads will read our minds and translate our ideas into words, sounds, and images. We will communicate with each other without talking, reading, or using gestures!

Emojis

Emojis (or other symbols) will substitute text and sounds in communication and become a new language. Words won't be necessary.

Content for Three Senses

Photos and videos won't have only words, images, and audio, but also a smell that will combine with the content of the message.

Holograms

Calls of the future will project a hologram of you to make the conversation more realistic.

Talking to Things

As well as communicating with humans, we will communicate with robots and artificial intelligences, too. Talking to machines will be more common and natural. You will probably spend more time talking to your car or refrigerator than to another person!

Will face-to-face communication disappear in the future? How do you feel about these predictions? Do you think they will come true?

3 5.02 **Read and listen to the article. Match the headings below with sentences 1–6.**

- Content for Three Senses
- Emojis
- ~~Holograms~~
- Smartphones
- Talking to Things
- Telepathy

1 These will make calls more real in the future.
Holograms ....

2 There will be implants and devices in our ears, eyes, and hands.
....

3 We will watch a cooking class video and smell the food.
....

4 Many conversations will be silent, but rich in vocabulary, sounds, and images.
....

5 Images will communicate information more effectively than words.
....

6 Conversations with a machine will be more common than with a person.
....

THINK!

Do you think advances in technology always make communication better?

WORKBOOK p.131

LANGUAGE IN CONTEXT

1 **Look at the examples below. Complete the sentences from the article.**

Simple Future

Affirmative (+)	Negative (–)	Questions (?)
I **will call** you later.	I **won't call** you again.	**Will** I **use** this app?
You **will send** a message.	You **won't send** a message.	**Will** you **download** this app?
He **will receive** an email.	He **won't communicate** with video.	**Will** he **text** me?
She **will translate** the text.	She **won't understand** the message.	**Will** she **send** me an email?
It **will be** better.	It **won't be** easy.	[4] __________ it __________ very different?
We [1] __________ Bluetooth devices in our ears and eyes. Smartphones [2] __________ part of our bodies.	We **won't have** a video chat today.	**Will** we **understand** the message?
	Words [3] __________ necessary.	**Will** they **call** me later?

2 **Remember the ideas in the article and circle the correct options.**

1 *We won't talk / Will we talk* to our cars in the future?
2 People *will use / won't use* smartphones like we use them today.
3 *It will be / Will it be* strange to communicate without words.
4 *It will be / Will it be* possible to smell the perfume in a commercial on TV?
5 I think the Internet *will be / won't be* the same in the future.

LOOK!
won't = will not

3 **Complete the text with *will* and the verbs in parentheses.**

I think the future of communication [1] will be (be) great. On the one hand, we [2] __________ (not meet) in real life because we [3] __________ (not leave) our houses very often. On the other hand, we [4] __________ (have) more options to talk to each other and keep in touch. We [5] __________ (make) friends from different countries. [6] __________ we __________ (speak) the same language? No, but we [7] __________ (understand) each other because apps [8] __________ (translate) our conversations into any language we want. Of course, we [9] __________ (not talk) to people like we do today. [10] __________ it __________ (be) better? Only time [11] __________ (tell).

USE IT!

4 **Work in pairs. Take turns making predictions about your life ten years from now. Talk about schools, food, and entertainment.**

Ten years from now, we won't go to school.

I agree. We will learn at home with virtual teachers.

WORKBOOK p.128 and p.130 PRACTICE EXTRA

LISTENING AND VOCABULARY

COMMUNICATION 2

1 **Look at the image of James and Sarah. What do you think they're talking about?**

2 5.03 **Listen to James and Sarah. Were your ideas in Exercise 1 correct?**

3 **Complete sentences 1–7 with the words below.**

• debate • describe • explain • say • ~~speak~~ • tell • translates

1 James doesn't think he can ......speak...... "dog."
2 There's an app that .... audio simultaneously.
3 Buddy wants to .... something to James.
4 James doesn't .... how the cat translator works.
5 Sarah thinks Buddy is trying to .... James to take him to the park.
6 People can .... in different languages and understand each other with the app.
7 James doesn't .... the cat translator exactly to Sarah, but he sends her the link.

4 5.04 **Listen, check, and repeat the words.**

5 5.03 **Listen to James and Sarah again. Then read the sentences and write *T* (true) or *F* (false).**

1 Buddy is James's dog. ...T...
2 There is an app that translates dog language. ......
3 According to scientists, dogs can't communicate. ......
4 When scientists invent a dog-translating app, James will use it. ......
5 You can get cat translators online. ......

WORKBOOK p.129

LANGUAGE IN CONTEXT

1 **Complete the sentences from the dialogue in the chart. Use the words and the Look! box below.**

- going to learn
- 'm going to
- to talk

Future with *be going to*: Affirmative (+)

I[1] ______________ take Buddy to the park today.
You**'re going to** install this app.
She**'s going to** download the photo.
Buddy**'s going** [2] ______________ to me and I'll understand him.
We**'re** [3] ______________ one day!
They**'re going to** speak to the teacher.

LOOK!

I'll (= I **will**) send you the link. (He decided now.)

I'm (= I **am**) **going to** to buy a phone. (He decided this previously.)

2 **Complete the sentences with the correct form of *be going to* and the verbs in parentheses.**

1 You *'re going to debate* this plan with me. (debate)
2 She ______________ me an email later. (send)
3 They ______________ how to use emojis correctly. (explain)
4 Claudia, Tereza, and I ______________ together on the weekend. (study)
5 Your friend Luis called. He ______________ back later. (call)

3 **Look at the images. Write sentences with the prompts using *be going to*.**

1

They / start / video chat
They're going to start a video chat.

2
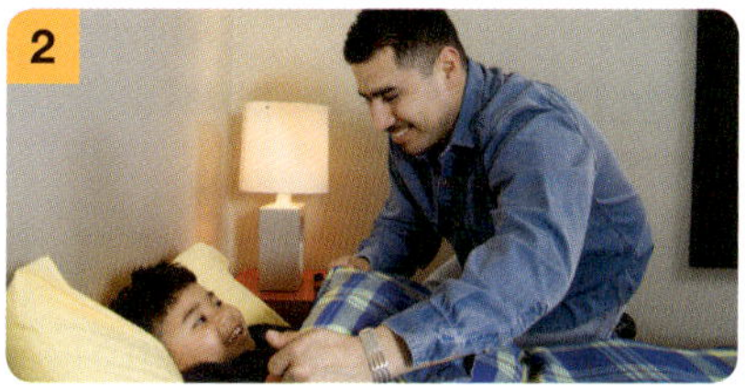
He / sleep
____

3

I / take / photo
____

4

You / explain / this app / me
____

5

We / take / our dog for a walk
____

USE IT!

I'm going to take a math test next week.

4 **Work in pairs. Take turns to tell your partner five things you're going to do next week.**

WORKBOOK p.128 and p.130   PRACTICE EXTRA

AROUND THE WORLD

IS SIGN LANGUAGE UNIVERSAL?

You are going to imagine a world with no sound. What is it like? How will you communicate without talking? Will you use images or maybe signs? That's right, we are going to talk about sign languages!

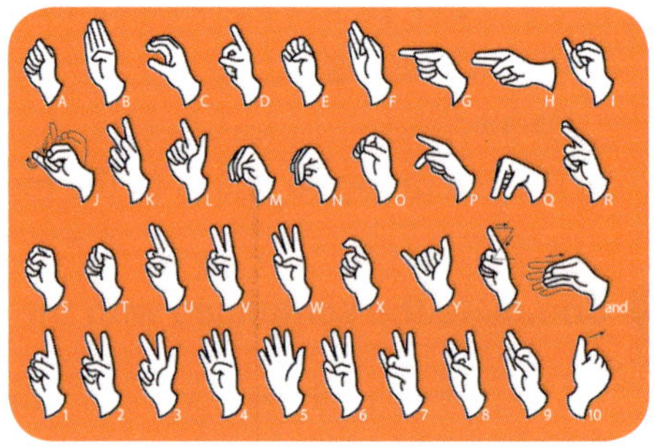

Sign languages use hand, face, and body movements for communication. They are not only for people with hearing difficulties, but also for people with Down syndrome, autism, and language difficulties. Can you believe there are over 135 different types of sign languages and many different sign language alphabets? In fact, even countries with the same spoken language do not use the same sign language. For example, the American Sign Language in the US and the British Sign Language in the UK do not use the same signs and have completely different grammar rules!

What is the explanation for these differences in sign languages? Groups of people from different areas created and developed their signs. But when they created these signs, globalization was not very common and people with hearing difficulties from different countries did not have to communicate with each other very often.

Sign languages change with time, too, of course. Take the word "telephone." Because of the changes in technology in the last 100 years, the sign for the word "telephone" changed, too. People create different signs to represent new things and concepts all the time.

Unfortunately, there are sign languages that are disappearing because not many people are learning and using them. For example, only about 40 people know Mardin Sign Language from Turkey. Young people are not learning the language, so it will become extinct in the near future, just like spoken languages.

1 **Look at the title, the images, and the first paragraph of the text. Then answer the questions.**

1 What are the people in the images doing?

....

2 Why are they doing this?

....

2 **Look at the second paragraph of the text. Find:**

1 three words related to the physical structure of humans.

.......hand....... ....

2 two words related to medical conditions.

....

3 two countries that speak the same language.

....

3 5.05 **Read and listen to the text. Then read the sentences and write *T* (true) or *F* (false).**

1 The objective of sign language is to communicate with hands, facial expressions and body movements. ....T....
2 There is only one sign language in the world. ....
3 There isn't a difference between sign language in the US and the UK. ....
4 Different sign languages have different grammar rules. ....
5 The Mardin Sign Language from Turkey is disappearing. ....

4 **Read the text again. Complete the sentences with the words below.**

• different • extinct • ~~listening~~ • vocabulary • world

1 Sign languages are not only for people with ....listening.... difficulties.
2 There are over 135 different types of sign language in the ....
3 People from .... cultures have their own sign languages.
4 Sign language .... is constantly changing.
5 Some sign languages will become .... if people stop using them.

WORDS IN CONTEXT

5 **Find words/phrases 1–4 in the text. Then match them with their explanations.**

1 in fact ....
2 not only … but also ....
3 of course ....
4 unfortunately ....

a We use it to present ideas that are similar or related.
b We use it to say that some information is not surprising or extraordinary.
c We use it to say something is sad, disappointing, or has a bad effect.
d We use it to give more details about an idea.

WEBQUEST

Learn more! Check (✓) *True* or *False*.

People with hearing difficulties often invent a special sign for their name.

◯ True ◯ False

THINK!

Some people can't hear and can't see. How do they communicate?

VIDEO

5.2

1 **How many words and languages are there in the world?**

2 **Why do some languages have lots of different words to describe one thing?**

SPEAKING

COMMUNICATING WHAT YOU WANT TO BUY

1 🔊 5.06 **Read and listen to Enzo and Camila. Where is Camila?**

Enzo Can I help you?
Camila Yes, I'm looking for a new **phone**.
Enzo How about this one?
Camila Hmm, do you have a **smaller** one?
Enzo Yes, what do you think about this **phone**?
Camila That's **awesome**! Does it have a **good camera**?
Enzo Of course! It's the **best camera** there is!
Camila Great! How much is it?

LIVING ENGLISH

2 **Read the dialogue in Exercise 1 again. Then complete the mini dialogues with the expressions below.**

- I'm looking for
- How much is it?
- What do you think about

1 A ....
B It's ten dollars.

2 A ....
this new app?
B It's awesome!

3 A ....
a happy emoji. Where are the emojis?
B They're here. Look!

3 🔊 5.07 **Listen, check, and repeat the expressions.**

6 🔊 5.06 **Listen to the dialogue again. Then practice with a partner.**

7 **Role play a new dialogue. Follow the steps.**

1 Change the words in **blue** to write a new dialogue in your notebook.
2 Practice your dialogue with a partner.
3 Present your dialogue to the class.

PRONUNCIATION

4 🔊 5.08 **Listen and pay attention to the pronunciation of the schwa /ə/.**

1 I'm looking for **a** new phone.
2 What do y**ou** think **a**bout this phone?
3 It's th**e** best camer**a** …

5 🔊 5.08 **Listen again and repeat.**

YOUR DIGITAL PORTFOLIO

Record your dialogue. Then upload it to your class digital portfolio.

PRACTICE EXTRA

6

EXTRAORDINARY LIVES

UNIT GOALS

- Talk about occupations and adjectives to describe people.
- Read about a difficult situation.
- Listen to a TV show interview.
- Learn about a medical genius.
- Write a biography.

THINK!

1 **Look at the photo. What do you think their lives are like?**

2 **Who do you think is an extraordinary person?**

VIDEO

6.1

1 **What makes people extraordinary? Name three reasons.**

2 **What difficult situations did Terezinha Guilhermina face?**

VOCABULARY IN CONTEXT

OCCUPATIONS

1 6.01 **Label the people with the correct occupation. Then listen, check, and repeat.**

- actor
- ~~athlete~~
- chef
- dancer
- engineer
- fashion designer
- inventor
- musician
- nurse
- politician
- writer

Images Videos Maps Shopping More Settings

extraordinary people and their occupations |

Serena Williams is an American tennis player. She is an amazing 1 athlete.

- Elvis Presley

2 ________________

- Clara Barton

3 ________________

- Leonardo da Vinci

4 ________________

- Penélope Cruz

5 ________________

- William Shakespeare

6 ________________

- Stella McCartney

7 ________________

- Franz Sacher

8 ________________

- Mikhail Baryshnikov

9 ________________

- Jacinda Ardern

10 ________________

- Nikola Tesla

11 ________________

2 **Look at the images and complete the sentences with the correct occupation from Exercise 1.**

1

2

3

4
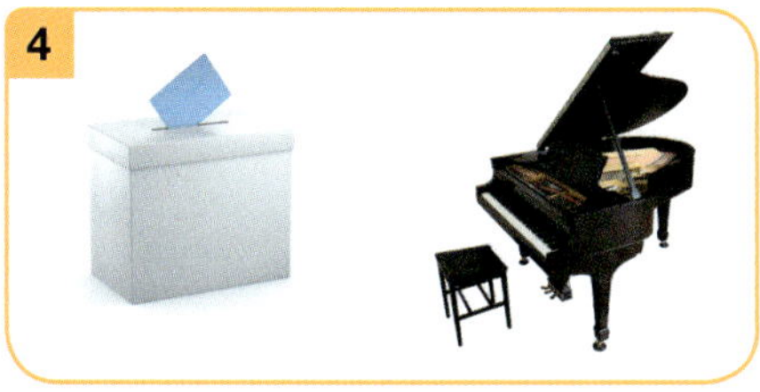

5

6

7

1 My dad works in the hospital. He's a ____nurse____. My mom creates clothes. She's a ________.

2 I work in the theater and I love moving to music. I'm an ________ and a ________.

3 My sister designs things and builds machines. She's going to be an ________. My brother makes incredible cakes. He's going to be a ________.

4 My uncle works for the government. He's a ________. My aunt can play the piano and sing. She's the ________ of the family.

5 My cousin loves all sports. She's an ________. She can run very fast!

6 My grandfather gave me a book of his stories for my birthday. He's a ________.

7 I like imagining things, like Leonardo da Vinci. I want to be an ________.

3 **Complete the chart with the name of another famous person you know for each occupation.**

Famous Person	*He/She is a/an ...*	Famous Person	*He/She is a/an ...*
________	actor	________	inventor
________	athlete	________	musician
________	chef	________	nurse
________	dancer	________	politician
________	engineer	________	writer
________	fashion designer		

USE IT!

4 **Work in pairs. Take turns choosing two of the occupations in the chart in Exercise 3 and guessing the names of your partner's famous people.**

She's an actor.

Is she Brazilian?

READING

Me
To: Dad
Subject: Miss you

Dear Dad,

I hope this finds you well. We all miss you a lot!
We're safe inside, don't worry. Mom is working from home now and she's cooking better than ever!
Grandma is fine in her apartment, too. We're going to start online yoga classes together!
But how about you, Dad? Sorry your phone isn't working. At least you have your laptop, right? Is your new phone going to arrive soon?
When are you going to come home? I hope you have a vacation after all this. Nurses need to rest, too. And your swimming practice? Are you going to go back to that? You're a great swimmer, Dad, don't stop!
Well, I'm sure about one thing: this pandemic is going to end. And I have so many plans for the future! I'm going to meet my friends every day, and we're going to go to the mall, go to the movies, play basketball ... so many things!
School is still closed, but classes online are OK. I miss my friends. I really want to see them. Meeting online is not the same. Believe it or not, I'm certain about two things. I'll be the best student in my class and I won't say bad things about school ever again!
Dad, I changed my mind: I'm not going to be a professional athlete anymore. I'm going to be a scientist and help the world fight public health problems. Wait and see!

Love,
Katie

1 **Who do you write emails to? Why?**

2 6.02 **Read and listen to the email. Answer questions 1 and 2 and check (✓) the correct answer to question 3.**

1 What is Katie's dad's occupation and where does he work?

----

2 Why didn't Katie text her dad?

----

3 What's the context of the email?

- ◯ Part of Katie's family is at home during a period of social isolation.
- ◯ There's a pandemic and Katie's dad is on vacation.
- ◯ Katie's family is now living in her grandma's home.

3 **Read the email again. Check (✓) the promises that Katie makes to her father.**

- ◯ She'll be the best student in her class.
- ◯ She won't say bad things about school anymore.
- ◯ She's going to take yoga classes with her grandma.
- ◯ She's going to do many different activities with her friends.

THINK!

Do you think Katie's dad is an extraordinary person? Do you think Katie is an extraordinary person? Why/Why not?

WORKBOOK p.135

LANGUAGE IN CONTEXT

1 **Look at the examples below. Complete the sentences from the email.**

Future with *be going to*			
Affirmative (+)	**Negative (–)**	***Yes/No* Questions (?)**	**Short Answers**
I'm **going to** 1 ...be... a scientist.	I'm **not** 3 .... a professional athlete.	**Am** I **going to** be a scientist?	Yes, I **am**. / No, I'**m not**.
You'**re going to** cook.	You'**re not going to** go to the mall.	4 .... you .... back to that?	Yes, you **are**. / No, you'**re not**.
He/She'**s going to** change.	He/She'**s not going to** win.	**Is** he/she **going to** arrive soon?	Yes, he/she **is**. / No, he/she/it'**s not**.
We/They'**re going to** 2 .... online yoga classes.	We/They'**re not going to** buy a new phone.	**Are** we/they **going to** play volleyball?	Yes, we/they **are**. / No, we/they'**re not**.
***Wh–* Questions (?)**			
What am I **going to** do?	**When** 5 .... home?	**Where are** we **going to** meet?	

2 **Rewrite the sentences in the correct negative or question form.**

1 She's going to speak at the conference. (–)
She's not going to speak at the conference.
2 I'm going to organize a picnic on Sunday. (–)
....
3 We're not going to go to the theater. (?)
....
4 He's not going to spend a lot of money. (?)
....
5 Is Olga going to write a poem? (–)
....

LOOK!

To make a *Wh–* question add a *Wh–* word before a *Yes/No* question.

When are you going to come home?

Where is she going to study?

3 **Complete the sentences with the correct form of *be going to* and the verbs below.**

• ~~compete~~ • dance • discover • help • sing

1 Alec ...'s not going to compete... at the national championship because he's sick.
2 .... Rebecca .... with her boyfriend at the prom?
3 Julie is in the hospital, so she .... her new song at the club.
4 Jonas and Bob .... their mom cook dinner because they have a test tomorrow.
5 I'm sure scientists .... a new medicine soon.

USE IT!

4 **Take turns asking about your partner's weekend plans and answering with information about what you are not going to do.**

What are you going to do on the weekend?

Well, I'm not going to study on Saturday.

WORKBOOK p.132 and p.134 PRACTICE EXTRA

LISTENING AND VOCABULARY

ADJECTIVES TO DESCRIBE PEOPLE

1 **Look at the image. What occupation does it show?**

2 6.03 **People in different occupations need different qualities. Complete the sentences with the words below. Then listen, check, and repeat the words.**

- available
- flexible
- ~~helpful~~
- reliable
- successful
- suitable

1 My dad's a nurse and he's always helping other people. He's the most ......helpful...... person I know.
2 She's famous now, but it took years of practice for her to be .... as a musician.
3 Important politicians have to be .... 24 hours a day.
4 We think your new and original ideas make you very .... for the job of an inventor.
5 Working as a chef makes you .... You need to make decisions very quickly.
6 You can count on engineers to be .... When they promise something, they'll do it.

3 6.04 **Listen to an interview with Diane about the qualities she needs for her occupation. Circle the correct options.**

1 Diane works at a *university* / *school*.
2 She works in *the local community* / *a different area*.
3 She sometimes works *late at night* / *early in the morning*.
4 People in her job need to love working with *young people* / *adults*.
5 She sometimes feels like a person working in a *restaurant* / *theater*.

4 6.04 **Listen to the interview again and put the adjectives to describe people in the order you hear them. Do you think Diane is an extraordinary person?**

a .... available
b .... flexible
c .... helpful
d .... reliable
e ...1... successful
f .... suitable

5 **Complete the chart with the words from Exercise 4. Then add two words from the list of personality adjectives on page 32.**

Adjectives Ending in *–able* or *–ible*	Adjectives Ending in *–ful*
available,	

WORKBOOK p.133

LANGUAGE IN CONTEXT

1 **Complete the sentences from the interview in the chart. Use the words/phrases below.**

- enough
- too many
- too much

Intensifiers	
There are [1] ______ hours in my schedule.	There's [3] ______ work.
There aren't [2] ______ hours in the day.	There's **enough** work for all of us.

2 **Circle the correct options.**

1 There are *too many* / *too much* pages to read.
2 The closet's very small. There's *enough* / *not enough* room for all our clothes.
3 There's *too many* / *too much* rice in this dish.
4 We didn't have *enough* / *not enough* time to finish the test.
5 The beach is crowded. There are *too many* / *too much* people.

3 **Complete the text with *too many* or *too much*.**

My sister is a chef. But the recipe she made for us on Sunday was a disaster! She put [1] too many onions and [2] ______ salt in it, so it didn't taste good. She cooked the pie for [3] ______ time, so it was hard. She invited [4] ______ people for lunch, so there wasn't enough food. I think there were [5] ______ young children in the kitchen when she was making the pie.

LOOK!

We use *too many* with countable nouns.

There are too many students in my class.

We use *too much* with uncountable nouns.

There's too much noise! I can't hear!

We use *enough* with countable and uncountable nouns. It means *sufficient*.

There aren't enough tomatoes for a salad.

There's enough milk for breakfast.

USE IT!

4 **Complete sentences 1–3 with information about you. Then take turns choosing your sentences with a partner and completing the chart with your partner's information.**

You	Your Partner
1 I have too much ______.	
2 There are too many ______.	
3 I don't have enough ______.	

I have too much homework.

WORKBOOK p.132 and p.134 PRACTICE EXTRA

ACROSS THE CURRICULUM

ETHICS

Home | Profile | Contact

Profile

David Rodriguez

Great Power

Do you know that line from a famous movie, "With great power comes great responsibility"? Well, David Rodriguez is a perfect example of this.

David was born in the US on July 17, 1993. He could walk and talk when he was only ten months old, and he could read and write when he was two. At seven all the other children of his age were playing games, learning to read, write, and do basic math, but not David. He already had responsibilities because of his exceptional gift. Considered a prodigy in his town, in 2000 he helped his dad with a surgery on a girl to help her and her family. Her parents' video of the surgery went viral. Later, he became the youngest student to go to high school in his community. He went to medical school at the age of 11 and got a degree in medicine.

What is David doing today? Enjoying his fame and making money? No way! He is a real genius in the area of medicine. He's specializing in bioengineering and focusing on a cure for cancer. When he was growing up, he read about many people suffering from cancer because they couldn't pay for the expensive treatment. This made David very sad, but it helped him find his goal in life. "I'm not going to rest," he says. "I'm going to help find a cure for cancer."

What about you? How are you going to use your power to make a difference in this vast, diverse, and unequal world?

1 **What could you do very well when you were a child? Can you still do it very well now? Share your answers with a partner.**

2 6.05 **Read and listen to the text. Circle the correct options.**

1 David learned to walk and talk in *1993* / *1994*.
2 He learned to read and write in *1995* / *1996*.
3 He helped a girl and her family in *2000* / *2001*.
4 He went to medical school in *2003* / *2004*.

3 **Check (✓) what helped David find his goal in life.**

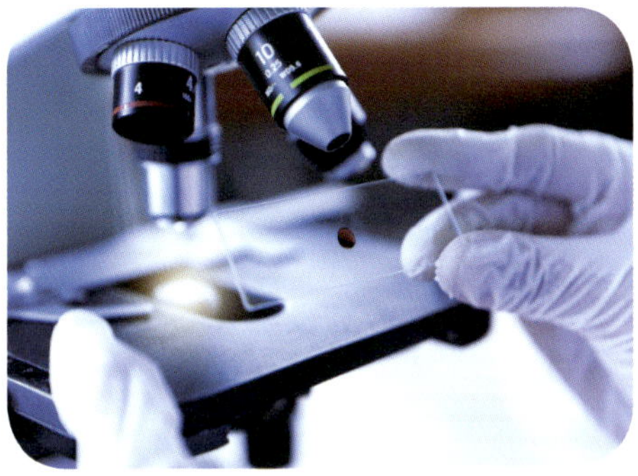

- ◯ the fact that people consider him a genius
- ◯ the sad reality around him
- ◯ the information that doctors make good money
- ◯ a cure for cancer that he learned in school
- ◯ his exceptional intelligence

WORDS IN CONTEXT

4 **Find these words in the text.**

1 a synonym for *talent* ....
2 a noun for a young person who is very talented at something ....
3 a synonym for *a medical operation* ....
4 a noun for what you get when you finish college ....
5 an adjective that means different in size, level, amount, etc. ....

THINK!

What things may be difficult for an extremely talented person?

WEBQUEST

Learn more! Check (✓) *True* or *False*.
Peter Parker's aunt says, "With great power comes great responsibility" in the movie *Spider-Man*.

◯ **True** ◯ **False**

VIDEO

6.2

1 **Why is it a good idea to start learning music at a young age?**
2 **What two qualities do professional musicians need to become excellent?**

WRITING

Nicola Benedetti

Nicola Benedetti is a famous Scottish musician. She was born on July 20, 1987, in West Kilbride, Scotland. She is one of the most influential classical artists of today.

She started learning the violin when she was four years old. At age ten, she went to the Yehudi Menuhin School, a school for young musicians.

Nicola is a very talented artist. However, she believes her talent comes from hard work.

She practices three to seven hours every day – sometimes there aren't enough hours in one day! She uses a very rare and expensive instrument, a Stradivarius violin from 1717.

As well as playing the violin beautifully, Nicola is passionate about music education. In 2019, she founded the Benedetti Foundation to unite, inspire, and educate young musicians and teachers.

1 **Look at the mini biography and underline information a–c.**

a the name of the person
b the date and place of birth
c the person's profession

2 6.06 **Read and listen to the text. Then match topics a–d with paragraphs 1–4.**

a two academic anecdotes ....
b why this person is extraordinary ....
c two facts about the present ....
d basic personal information ....

3 **Study the example in the LOOK! box. Then circle two defining phrases in the mini biography.**

LOOK!

Defining Phrases

She was born on July 20, 1987 in West Kilbride, **a small town in the southwest of Scotland**.

4 **Write a mini biography of an artist you admire.**

1 Choose an artist to write about.
2 Collect information about the artist.
3 Find or draw an image to illustrate your mini biography.
4 Write the first version of your mini biography. Use vocabulary from Unit 3.

5 **Switch your mini biography with a classmate and check their work. Use the checklist below.**

- ○ title and image
- ○ date of birth, place of birth, and profession
- ○ clear sections: personal, academic, present, and interesting additional information
- ○ defining phrases, intensifiers

YOUR DIGITAL PORTFOLIO

Edit your mini biography. Then publish it. Upload it to the class portfolio for everyone to see!

REVIEW
UNITS 5 AND 6

VOCABULARY

1 Match images a–e with sentences 1–5.

1 I really enjoy face-to-face conversations with my friends. ...e...
2 I like to add emojis to my text messages. ....
3 They're using English to communicate. It's their common language. ....
4 She's texting her dad. ....
5 They're having a video chat! With virtual communication, they can have a party! ....

2 Complete the sentences with the words below.

• debate • describe • explain • tell • ~~translate~~

1 I can't speak Spanish. I don't know how to ...translate... this sentence!
2 Can you .... what he looked like? Was he tall?
3 Let me .... the instructions to you one more time.
4 Teachers often .... the use of cell phones in class.
5 Finn can .... you when the teacher is coming.

3 Match 1–9 with a–i.

1 actor ...b...	4 dancer	7 musician ....
2 athlete	5 engineer	8 nurse ....
3 chef	6 inventor	9 writer ....

4 Circle the correct options.

1 Valerie is *suitable* / *reliable*. You can count on her to help you with the surprise party.
2 Greg is a *successful* / *flexible* athlete. He won two championships last year.
3 Jon and Ling are really *flexible* / *reliable*. They don't have a problem with change.
4 Dr. Soares is always *available* / *successful*. Call her when you don't feel well.
5 Naim is very *available* / *helpful* and strong. He can help you with the heavy chairs.
6 Brenda was the most *helpful* / *suitable* candidate for the job.

LANGUAGE IN CONTEXT

5 **Look the chart. Write questions and answers about what the people will do using the simple future.**

Anthony	call his friends ? (✓)	text his brother (X)
Nathan	text Gina ? (✓)	use emojis (✓)
José	study to be a chef ? (X)	go to France (X)
Marie	go to the park ? (✓)	meet her friends (✓)
Claire	read a book in English ? (✓)	translate the story (X)

1 Will Anthony call his friends? Yes, he will. He won't text his brother.

2 ....

3 ....

4 ....

5 ....

6 **Write questions about the underlined information in answers 1–5.**

1 We're going to go shopping on Saturday.

When are you going to go shopping?

2 I'm going to have a salad for lunch.

....

3 My best friend is going to be at home on the weekend.

....

4 My classmates are going to arrive at school at 7 a.m. tomorrow.

....

5 My cousin is going to be happy because our whole family will be at her party tonight.

....

7 **Complete the sentences with *too many*, *too much*, or (*not*) *enough*.**

1 When I drink too much coffee, I can't sleep.

2 There are .... books for everyone. You will need to share.

3 He uses .... emojis. His messages are full of them.

4 I think there is .... graffiti in this town. There are images everywhere.

5 We're very excited! We have .... money to buy a car!

CHECK YOUR PROGRESS

I CAN...

- talk about communication.
- use the simple future.
- talk about occupations and adjectives to describe people.
- use the future with *be going to* and intensifiers.

LEARN TO LEARN

Transparent Words

Some words may be similar in Portuguese and in English. Sometimes words are the same, as in *radio* (radio), and sometimes they're different, as in *pretender* (intend) and *fingir* (pretend). Words that have similar forms and meaning are called **transparent words**, and they can increase your vocabulary!

7 THIS IS FUN!

UNIT GOALS

- Talk about different types of video channels and free-time activities.
- Read an instant message chat.
- Listen to a voice chat.
- Learn about an old popular story.
- Make and react to arrangements.

THINK!

1 What is your favorite free-time activity?
2 Why do people need entertainment?

VIDEO 7.1

1 When did people start using the screen?
2 Name three types of on-screen entertainment from the video.

VOCABULARY IN CONTEXT

VIDEO CHANNELS

1 **Complete the descriptions in the list with the words below.**

- beauty
- cooking
- gaming
- health and fitness
- reviews
- science and tech
- unboxing
- ~~vlogger~~

MY FAVORITE ONLINE VIDEO CHANNELS

By Patricia Mendes

1 It's Mia Queen

Mia Shelly is my favorite ___vlogger___! She posts videos of her everyday life.

2 X-Y-A-DOWN-RIGHT

The best ______ channel! Don is a professional player famous for his Minecraft videos.

3 Out in the Open

______ videos are nice to watch. On this channel, they open and test new products.

4 Ava de la Croix

A ______ channel with great tutorials from fashion to makeup and cosmetics!

5 Scientific Teenager

A ______ channel with a lot of videos about physics, chemistry, and biology.

6 Dissiz Food

This ______ channel has everything for your kitchen and food interests!

7 The Test Guy

In his ______ channel, Samuel tries everything from movies to products and gives his opinions.

8 Go Ellie Go

I don't watch many ______ channels, but Ellie makes exercises and nutrition fun.

2 7.01 **Listen, check, and repeat.**

3 **Now match the type of channels in Exercise 1 with this content.**

a people playing and talking about a new video game ...2...
b yoga lessons ....
c an opinion about a new camera ....
d a person talking about a trip to Peru ....
e opening a new cell phone ....
f a recipe for a chocolate cake ....
g instructions on how to wash your face at night ....
h the story of space exploration ....

4 **Look at the playlist below. Write the types of channels and their names from Exercise 1.**

		Name of Channel	Type of Channel	Theme Song
A		....	....	....
B		....	....	....
C		....	....	....
D		It's Mia Queen	vlogger	....
E		....	....	....
F		....	....	....
G		....	....	....
H		....	....	....

5 **Work in pairs. Choose a theme song for each channel and complete the playlist in Exercise 4.**

USE IT!

What's your favorite gaming channel?

It's Online Gamers.

6 **Talk about your favorite channels with a partner.**

READING

1 **Look at the messages. Then discuss your answers to the questions with a partner.**

1 When is it better to send text messages to your friends? When is it better to send audio or video messages?

Hey, Jane! Can you talk?

I'm taking care of my little brother. It's better to text.

Oh, OK. I liked your recent article about channels. I'd like to share my list with you. Would you like to see it?

Yes, I'd love to. Hearing about new channels is cool!

I follow some channels you don't. For example, Cheeza Liz. Do you know her?

Hmm ... I don't think so.

She's a health, fitness, and beauty vlogger from Canada. She's so funny!

Why funny?

She always makes me laugh! She's really not good at giving instructions. Last week, she broke a chair during an exercise!!

LOL. I'll definitely check it out.

Yesss!!!

Pat, what about reviews channels? I love them.

Me 2! There's Sam Beetz. He's the best IMO. He's like really, really big in Australia.

Oh, I don't like him. I don't believe anything he says.

All his opinions are so fake. But some people believe him. Just because you see something on a video, it doesn't mean it's real.

2 7.02 **Read and listen to the messages. Then read the sentences and write *T* (true) or *F* (false).**

1 Pat wants to speak to Jane. T
2 Jane and Pat have the same favorite online video channels. ____
3 Only one channel in Pat's list is from an English-speaking country. ____
4 Pat probably believes what Sam Beetz says in his reviews channel. ____

3 **Read the chat again. Number the words/phrases below (1–6) with the icons.**

____ agree with	____ be very pleased	____ be surprised
1 ~~laugh~~	____ laugh and cry	____ like/love a lot

1 2 3 4 5 6

THINK!

Do you think the information on the Internet is true? Why / Why not?

WORKBOOK p.139

LANGUAGE IN CONTEXT

1 **Look at the examples below. Complete the sentences from the instant message chat.**

Polite Offers: *would like to / would love to*		
Affirmative (+)	***Yes/No* Questions (?)**	**Short Answers**
I'd [1] .... to share my list with you.	[2] .... you **like** to see it?	Yes, I'**d** [3] .... to. / No, thank you.
I **would love** to help you with your homework.	**Would** you **like** to watch a movie with us?	Yes, we'**d like** to. / No, thank you.
We **would like** to show you our new home.	**Would** she **like** to test these new products?	Yes, she **would**. / No, she **wouldn't**.
We'**d love** to send you some songs.	**Would** they **like** to post their videos?	Yes, they **would**. / No, they **wouldn't**.

2 **Put the words in the correct order to make sentences or questions.**

1 watch / like to / videos / every day / about cookies / I'd / .
I'd like to watch videos about cookies every day.

2 meet / vlogger / we'd / your favorite / love to / .
....

3 new video / you / like / would / to watch / my / ?
....

4 to her / channel / you / I / would like / to subscribe / .
....

5 you / like / with me / video games / to play / would / ?
....

LOOK!

***Would like* and *want* mean the same thing, but we use *would like* in more formal and polite conversations.**

I want to talk to you.

I'd (**would**) **like** to talk to you.

3 **Answer the questions.**

1 Would you like to watch a movie now? If so, what movie?
....

2 Would you like to be a famous Instagrammer? If so, what type?
....

3 Would you like to start a channel on the Internet? If so, what type?
....

USE IT!

Would you like to play soccer?

I'd love to.

4 **Work in groups. Take turns suggesting things to do on the weekend.**

WORKBOOK p.136 and p.138 PRACTICE EXTRA

LISTENING AND VOCABULARY

FREE-TIME ACTIVITIES

1 7.03 **Label images a–f with the phrases below. Then listen, check, and repeat.**

- eat out
- ~~go to a concert~~
- have a sleepover
- play in a band
- throw a party
- watch series

a

1

go to a concert

b

c

d

e

f

2 7.04 **Listen to a voice chat between two friends. Number the activities in Exercise 1 in the order you hear them (1–6).**

3 7.04 **Listen again. Write *T* (true) or *F* (false).**

1 Sarah is typing, and Eve is answering with audio messages. T
2 Sarah and Eve have different plans for Friday. ......
3 Sarah will have a sleepover on Saturday. ......
4 It's Eve's grandpa's birthday on Saturday. ......
5 Sarah won't go to the party at Eve's house. ......
6 Sarah accepted Eve's invitation for lunch. ......

4 **Read the messages and write the activities from Exercise 1.**

I really love spaghetti. — 1 eat out

My birthday is next week! — 2 ......

I want to see *The Teens* play live! — 3 ......

Bring your pajamas, OK? — 4 ......

I can't wait to watch the season finale! — 5 ......

Steve, who taught you that guitar solo? — 6 ......

WORKBOOK p.137

LANGUAGE IN CONTEXT

1 Complete the sentences from the voice chat in the chart. Use the words and the LOOK! box below.

• going • not • 're • you

Present Progressive for Future Plans, Appointments, and Arrangements

Affirmative (+)	Negative (–)
I'**m** [1] ______ **out** with some friends on Friday. You'**re traveling** next week. He/She'**s giving** a presentation tomorrow. We [2] ______ **practicing** this Friday. They'**re coming** to the city in two months.	I'**m not going** to the gym on Sunday. You'**re not watching** series on Friday. He/She'**s not studying** tonight. We'**re** [3] ______ **doing** that this week. They'**re not coming** this Saturday.
***Yes/No* Questions (?)**	**Short Answers**
Am I **watching** series this weekend? **Are** [4] ______ **doing** anything this afternoon? **Is** he/she **going** to a **concert on Saturday**? **Are** we **having** a test tomorrow? **Are** they **throwing** a party for you tomorrow?	Yes, I **am**. / No, I'**m not**. Yes, you **are**. / No, you'**re not**. Yes, he/she **is**. / No, he/she'**s not**. Yes, we **are**. / No, we'**re not**. Yes, they **are**. / No, they'**re not**.

2 Complete the sentences with the correct form of the present progressive of the verbs in parentheses.

1 I *'m hanging out* with my friends and cousins this weekend. (hang out)
2 We ______ the bus this afternoon. (not take)
3 ______ Luciana ______ her book tonight? (read)
4 Tyrone ______ math tomorrow. (study)
5 ______ we ______ video games next Saturday? (play)
6 Alyssa ______ a birthday party later today. (throw)

LOOK!

My grandparents are coming **now**. (present action)

My grandparents are coming **this Saturday**. (future plan)

3 Check (✓) the prompts in the chart that are true for you.

	You	Your Partner
1 go to the movies / next Sunday		
2 eat pizza / for dinner today		
3 watch series / Saturday night		
4 eat out / tomorrow		
5 throw a party / this month		

USE IT!

Are you going to the movies next Sunday?

Yes, I am.

4 Work in pairs. Take turns asking questions and complete the chart for your partner. Are you doing the same things?

WORKBOOK p.136 and p.138 PRACTICE EXTRA

AROUND THE WORLD

My Reading Journal Blog

Hi, I'm Vibhuti.
This blog is about all the things I read.
Please comment!

This is a very old story from India or from China. No one really knows. The version I read online is about a girl named Chen Mei, who lived in a small village with her family.

The Cracked Pot

Every day Chen Mei walked from her village to a distant spring to collect clean, fresh water. It was a long walk, but she enjoyed it. She carried two pots, one on each side of her body. One of them was old and cracked, while the other one was perfect and new.

She always filled both pots with water from the spring, but when she got home the cracked pot was always only half full. The perfect pot was proud of its job, but the cracked pot was sad about its imperfection.

One day, when they were at the spring, the cracked pot spoke and said, "I feel terrible! Every day, I lose half of my water because of this crack in my side! I'd like to be new again."

The girl looked kindly at the cracked pot and said, "I want to show you something today. Would you like to see it?"

"Yes," said the cracked pot, so the girl started walking back.

Along the way, Chen Mei said, "Look at the flowers on your side of the road.

Can you smell them? Look at the other side. There aren't any flowers."

"That's true," said the cracked pot, "My side of the road has flowers, but the other doesn't. Why is that?"

"Because of your imperfection, I planted flower seeds on your side of the road, and every day, while we were going back, you watered them," Chen Mei explained. "These are the pretty flowers you can see at home. My mother loves them! The beauty we enjoy is thanks to you! Would you really like to be new again?"

I think Chen Mei's attitude was fantastic! She knew how to respect the pot's imperfection, and that made the difference!

Comments

Bookworm
6 hours ago
We're all cracked pots. But our cracks and imperfections make our lives together so different and rich.

shoot_the_star
20 hours ago
Old stories are boring. Ugh! Who wants to read? Video is the thing.

librat_brochure
2 days ago
I'm sharing this. So cool! Some people really respect others as they are. My math teacher is like that. I'd like to be like him. He sees the good side in everybody.

You

1 **Imagine you have a blog. What would you like to talk about in your blog? Discuss your ideas with a partner.**

2 **Look at the blog. What does Vibhuti do in her blog? Check (✓) the correct answer.**

In her blog, Vibhuti …

- ◯ tells a story that she read online and she mentions the writer's name: Chen Mei.
- ◯ tells an imaginary story to teach her readers a lesson about people's imperfections.
- ◯ uses her own words to tell her readers about an interesting old story she read online.

3 7.05 **Read and listen to the blog. What did Chen Mei do in the story? Check (✓) the correct answer.**

In the story, Chen Mei …

- ◯ didn't care which hand she held each pot in, because the important thing was to take the water home.
- ◯ respected the cracked pot and wanted to use the fact that it was cracked to create something good.
- ◯ always carried the cracked pot on the same side of her body, with the perfect pot on the other because it was more comfortable.

WORDS IN CONTEXT

4 **Check (✓) the correct image for words 1–4.**

1 cracked

a  ◯

b  ◯

2 proud

a 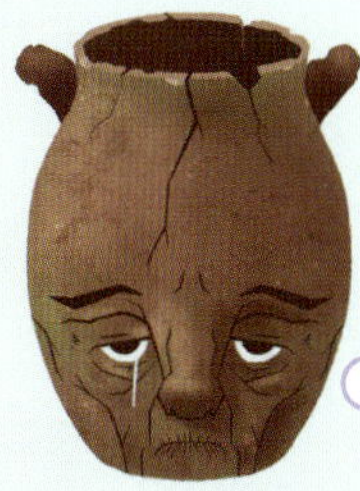 ◯

b  ◯

3 seeds

a  ◯

b  ◯

4 spring

a  ◯

b  ◯

5 **Read the blog comments and answer the questions.**

1 Which comment doesn't agree with Vibhuti's perspective?

....

2 Which comment do you agree with more? Why?

....

3 Write your comment on Vibhuti's blog under the three comments.

WEBQUEST

Learn more! Check (✓) *True* or *False*.

The cracked pot is an important element of a famous online game.

◯ **True** ◯ **False**

THINK!

How did you react to Vibhuti's blog and to the story? Why? Share your comment with a partner.

VIDEO

7.2

1 **Why is India's movie industry called Bollywood?**

2 **What are the typical characteristics of Bollywood movies?**

SPEAKING

MAKING AND REACTING TO ARRANGEMENTS

1 7.06 **Read and listen to Vitor and Henrique. Look at the image. Where do you think they are?**

Vitor: Next **Wednesday** is the series finale of **Obelisk**. Do you want to watch it together?

Henrique: Sounds good. We could probably just order some pizza.

Vitor: Great idea! We could have like, some **snacks** and **drinks**, too. I'm going to get some **popcorn**, **chocolate**, and **soda**.

Henrique: OK, sounds like a plan.

LIVING ENGLISH

2 **Read the dialogue in Exercise 1 again. Then complete the diagrams with the expressions below.**

- ~~Do you want to ...?~~
- Sounds good.
- Great idea!
- We could have ...
- I'm going to ...
- We could probably just ...
- OK, sounds like a plan.

Making Arrangements

Do you want to ...?

....

....

....

Reacting to Arrangements

....

....

....

3 7.07 **Listen, check, and repeat the expressions.**

PRONUNCIATION

4 7.08 **Listen and pay attention to the pronunciation of *want to* /ˈwaː.nə/ and *going to* /ˈgaː.nə/.**

/ˈwaː.nə/
Do you **want to** watch it together?

/ˈgaː.nə/
I'm **going to** get some popcorn, chocolate, and soda.

5 7.08 **Listen again and repeat the sentences.**

6 7.06 **Listen to the dialogue again. Then practice with a partner.**

7 **Role play a new dialogue. Follow the steps.**

1. Change the words in **blue** and write a new dialogue in your notebook.
2. Practice your dialogue with a partner.
3. Present your dialogue to the class.

YOUR DIGITAL PORTFOLIO

Record your dialogue. Then upload it to your class digital portfolio.

PRACTICE EXTRA

8

ONE WORLD

UNIT GOALS

- Talk about immigration.
- Read a letter to a future self.
- Listen to audio messages.
- Learn about immigration.
- Write an email.

THINK!

1 Are there any immigrants in your community? Where do they come from?

2 Why do people decide to leave their countries?

VIDEO

8.1

1 Name two things from the video that are becoming more similar across the world.

2 What is helping to create a single global culture?

VOCABULARY IN CONTEXT

IMMIGRATION

1 **Complete Femi's story diagram with the words below.**

- border
- feel at home
- ~~immigrants~~
- live abroad
- passports
- permanent residents
- reside
- visas

My Family's Dream Trip to Canada

I come from a family of [1] ______immigrants______. My grandparents were from Nigeria.

One day, they decided that they wanted to [2] ______________________. They wanted to give their children a better life.

They wanted to [3] ______________________ permanently in Canada. They wanted to become [4] ______________________.

After some time, they got their [5] ______________________. They could leave Nigeria.

They arrived at the [6] ______________________ with their [7] ______________________ and their dream of a new life.

In the beginning, it wasn't easy, but they [8] ______________________ in Canada now.

2 8.01 **Listen, check, and repeat the words.**

3 **Complete the diagrams with the words below.**

- immigrants
- live abroad
- ~~passports~~
- reside
- visas

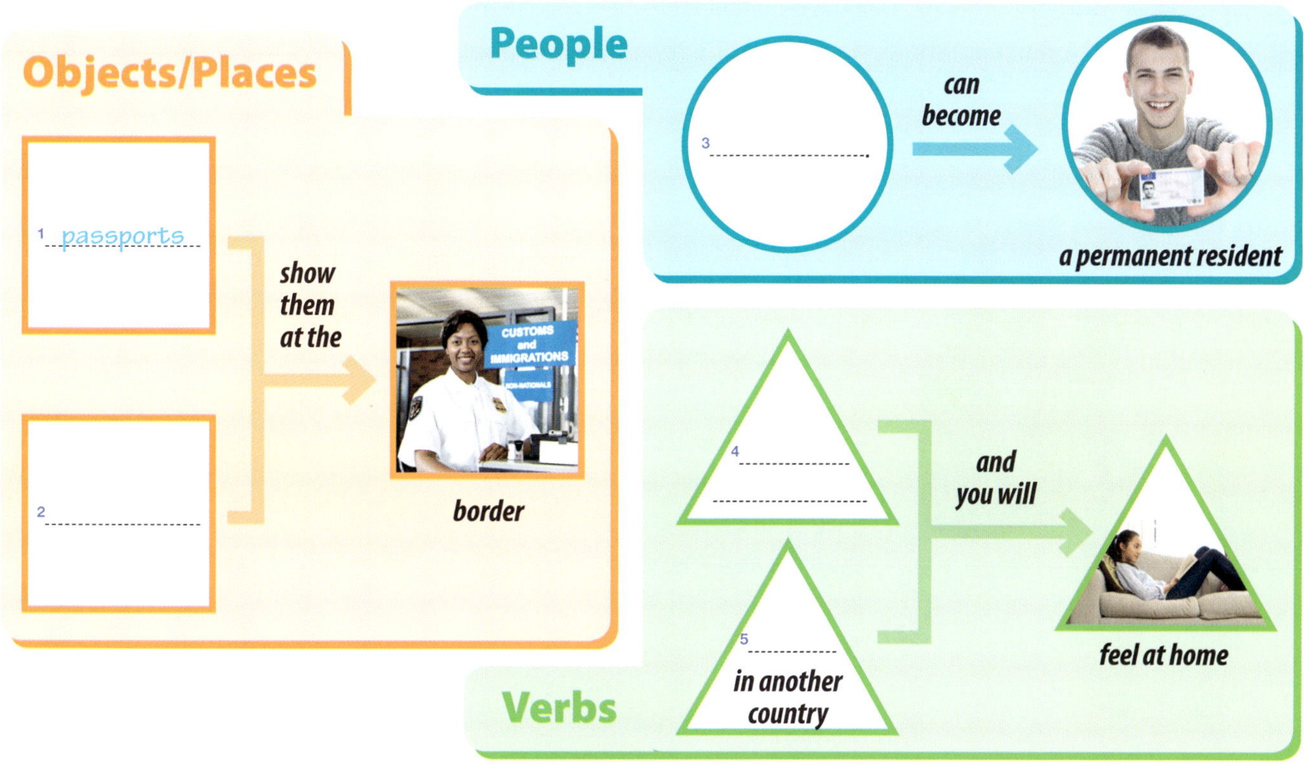

4 **Complete the sentences with the words from Exercise 1. Use the singular form of the nouns.**

1 Today my mother got her ...passport... and ....
2 Juan and Laura decided to leave Portugal and go to .... ten years ago. Now they really .... in Brazil.
3 Every .... needs to show his or her documents at the ....
4 My brother wants to .... in Quebec, Canada. He wants to become a .... in the future.

USE IT!

5 **Check (✓) the information that is true for you. Correct the false information. Then compare your information with a partner.**

◯ I have a passport.

....

◯ I have a visa to the United States.

....

◯ I live near the border with another country.

....

◯ When I'm at my friend's house I feel at home.

....

◯ Some of my family lives abroad.

....

READING

1 **What feelings and expectations do you think a teenager has about going to live in another country? Discuss your ideas with a partner.**

Dear Future Me,

Mom has a new job. Great, right? Except, it's in Australia! Yes, we're leaving the United States to live on the other side of the world. So, when I open this letter three years from now, how will my life be? Will we be happy in Sydney? Will we still be there?

I feel really anxious. The guys who hang out with me at school support me a lot. They say Australia is an awesome place. The weather is warm. But I don't know ... My hometown, Homewood, is an area that I feel safe in, and I can't imagine life away from our home on Cedar Road, the library around the corner, the snow every winter ... Here I have friends that are always there for me, especially Sue and Greg. Will I ever see them again? Well, at least they say Australians also play the game that inspires me: basketball. We'll see about that.

I'm going to do my best to be happy and help Mom, because this job is very important to her. Everything is going to be all right, but I'm sure I'm going to miss South Chicago. Please tell me I will be fine.

xoxo,

Dinah

2 8.02 **Read and listen to the text. Check (✓) the correct phrase to complete the sentence.**

In her letter to her future self, Dinah ...

- ◯ asks the reasons why she has to move to a land on the other side of the planet.
- ◯ expresses doubts about the future and sadness for the things that she will leave behind.
- ◯ shows anxiety because she knows life in a new country will be worse than in her hometown.

3 **Read the text again. Then read the sentences and write *T* (true) or *F* (false).**

1 Dinah and her mom are going to live in the capital of Australia. F

2 Dinah is going to destroy the letter before she leaves the US. ....

3 Dinah doesn't enjoy sports. ....

4 The library is near Dinah's house in the US. ....

5 Dinah's mom will leave Homewood because of a work opportunity. ....

4 **Check (✓) the best description of how Dinah feels about to going to Australia.**

- ◯ dramatic and irrational
- ◯ negative and emotional
- ◯ optimistic and happy
- ◯ positive but sentimental

THINK!

What's nice about writing a letter to yourself and opening it after a few years?

WORKBOOK p.143

LANGUAGE IN CONTEXT

1 **Look at the example and the LOOK! box below. Complete the sentences from Dinah's letter.**

Defining Relative Clauses with *who* and *that*		
The guys support me a lot. The guys hang out with me at school.	The guys [1] ___who___ **hang out with me at school** support me a lot.	**who** is for **people**
Australians play the game. The game inspires me: basketball. Here I have friends. Friends are always there for me.	Australians play the game [2] ______ **inspires me: basketball**. Here I have friends [3] ______ **are always there for me**.	**that** is for **people**, **animals**, and **things**

2 **Match 1–5 with a–e.**

1 My town's librarian is a person ___c___
2 Sydney is a city ______
3 I have some friends ______
4 What's the name of the sport ______
5 A letter to a future you is something ______

a who told me people play basketball in Australia.
b that you will open in the future.
c who always shows me good books to read.
d that you play every day?
e that is on the other side of the world.

3 **Write one sentence using the two sentences and *who* or *that*.**

1 They will move to a different region. The region offers job opportunities.
They will move to a different region that offers job opportunities.
2 I met new people. The people speak English.
______
3 They need to find a company. The company has flights to Australia.
______
4 Our ancestors were brave people. They came from Europe.
______
5 Brazil is a great country. Brazil welcomes immigrants.
______

LOOK!
A defining relative clause gives essential details about a noun.
This is the letter **that** I wrote last year.

USE IT!

4 **Work in pairs. Take turns describing the words below with a partner.**

- a cell phone
- a person's best friend
- an immigrant
- traveling abroad

An immigrant is a person who ...

LISTENING AND VOCABULARY

WORDS WITH PREFIXES

1 **Dinah lives in Sydney now. She and her friend Greg from Chicago often communicate by phone. Check (✓) the words you think you will hear in their audio messages.**

- ◯ bike
- ◯ Chicago
- ◯ country
- ◯ here
- ◯ like
- ◯ miss
- ◯ money
- ◯ school
- ◯ together
- ◯ weekend

2 8.03 **Listen to the audio messages and check your answers.**

3 8.03 **Listen to the messages again. Write the opposite of words 1–6.**

1 agree disagree
2 like ....
3 patient ....
4 possible ....
5 happy ....
6 kind ....

4 8.04 **Listen, check, and repeat the opposites.**

5 **Read the sentences and write *T* (true) or *F* (false).**

1 Dinah thought of Greg when she was standing in line. T
2 Greg and Dinah were at the Skydeck in Chicago last spring. ....
3 Dinah was right about her new life in Sydney. ....
4 Dinah now lives in a comfortable house. ....
5 Dinah is doing a lot of bike tours. ....

6 **Complete sentences 1–3 using your own words. Then compare your sentences with a partner.**

1 In general, people in my family dislike ....
2 I think it's impossible to ....
3 My best friend becomes impatient when ....

WORKBOOK p.141

LANGUAGE IN CONTEXT

1 **Complete the sentences from the audio messages in the chart using *who* or *which*. Use the LOOK! box to help you.**

Non-defining Relative Clauses with *who* and *which*
Greg, **who** lives in Chicago, is my best friend.
Our apartment, **which** is in Sydney, is very comfortable.
We went up the Sydney Tower, [1] .... is the tallest building here, to take pictures.
Sue, [2] .... really hates lines, had a bad moment.

2 **Complete the sentences with non-defining relative clauses. Use the information below.**

- He is a software designer.
- It has 110 floors.
- It is my favorite month.
- ~~It is the biggest city in Australia.~~
- They come from all parts of the world.

1 Sydney, which is the biggest city in Australia, is on the east coast of Australia.

2 Willis Tower, ..., is the third tallest building in the US.

3 My father, ..., likes to play video games on weekends.

4 February, ..., has 29 days every four years.

5 Immigrants, ..., often learn new languages.

3 **Write one sentence with a non-defining relative clause using the two sentences and *who* or *which*.**

1 Laura speaks English and Spanish. Laura lives in Australia.
Laura, who lives in Australia, speaks English and Spanish.

2 Last week, I bought my new cell phone. The cell phone takes great photos.
....

3 My favorite cars are Ferraris. Ferraris are Italian.
....

4 Mr. Garcia is going to visit Peru next year. Mr. Garcia is my history teacher.
....

5 Greg sent me a text message. Greg loves social media.
....

LOOK!

Non-defining relative clauses give extra information about a noun. Use commas to separate the non-defining relative clause.

Dinah, **who** is Greg's friend, lives in Sydney.

USE IT!

4 **Work in pairs. Describe the images 1–4 using non-defining relative clauses. Then compare your sentences with a partner.**

1 
My English dictionary

2 
My brother's soccer ball

3 
My cousin Catalina

4 
My cat Tabby

WORKBOOK p.140 and p.142 PRACTICE EXTRA

ACROSS THE CURRICULUM

SOCIAL STUDIES

IS IMMIGRATION GOOD FOR A COUNTRY?

BY MARK DOLLEN

Immigrants leave the south to go north, or the west to go east – they travel in all directions. Around the world, there are about **230 million** people who left their home country, but no matter where they go, they always take their culture with them. And that is good! Sharing cultures makes countries richer in so many ways.

1 New people mean new ideas. Immigrants bring with them their own expertise, traditions, cuisine, and art. This contributes to a country's own culture and enriches it.

2 More people working can make the economy grow. Immigrants have different occupations and different types of jobs. Some start their own businesses.

3 Immigrants help the community by paying taxes, which the government uses to provide public services.

4 When immigrants cross borders, people share their distinct cultures and develop new friendships. All these are steps toward making a more integrated, open, and empathetic world.

People leave their countries for different reasons: to look for better work opportunities, to reunite with family, to follow a dream, to escape from a conflict. But in all cases, they are always looking for a better life.

1 **Look at the title of the text and the images. Work in pairs. Discuss the questions.**

1 What do you see in the images?
2 Student A: think of arguments to answer yes to the question in the title. Student B: think of arguments to answer no. Can you convince your partner?

2 8.05 **Read and listen to the text. Does the author agree or disagree that immigration is good for a country? How do you know from the text?**

3 **Read the text again and answer the questions.**

1 Which tradition in your community comes from a different culture?
2 What dish in your country comes from a different nation?
3 Do you agree with the statement, "Immigrants influence the language of a country"? If so, give examples.
4 What does the author mean by "an empathetic world"?

WORDS IN CONTEXT

4 **Complete the sentences with the words below.**

• cuisine • expertise • steps • taxes

1 My grandpa has a lot of .... in math.
2 The government will pay for new schools by increasing ....
3 We need to take .... to reduce pollution.
4 The restaurant specializes in Japanese ....

THINK!

Why is it sometimes difficult for people from different cultures to understand each other?

WEBQUEST

Learn more! Check (✓) *True* or *False*.
France receives more immigrants than other countries.

○ True ○ False

VIDEO

8.2

1 Why is traditional food important to most people?
2 List the dishes you remember from the video.

WRITING

4 : 54 p.m.

me
to Mustafa

October 15

[1]Hi Mustafa!

[2]How are things? You're going to live in my neighborhood! You'll love it! The park that is near my house is beautiful and has a big lake. There's a community center, too. You'll meet new friends there.

[3]There's a restaurant called Turkish Delights, which sells delicious food from your country. I'm sure you'll feel at home because many customers are from Turkey.

[4]I want to introduce you to my family and friends. I'm very happy to know you're coming.

I can't wait to meet you next week!

George

1 8.06 **Read and listen to the email. Who are George and Mustafa? Check (✓) the correct sentence.**

◯ George and Mustafa are probably old friends.
◯ George and Mustafa are probably new friends.

2 Read the email again. Check (✓) the reason for George's email.

◯ to help Mustafa find places to eat Turkish food
◯ to show Mustafa interesting places to have fun
◯ to help Mustafa become familiar with the neighborhood
◯ to make Mustafa feel comfortable in his new school

3 Match a–d with parts 1–4 of the email.

a greeting ....
b details about a specific place in town ....
c closing paragraph ....
d general description of the neighborhood ....

4 Study the LOOK! box. Then circle another greeting expression and underline the goodbye phrase in the email.

5 Write an email to a friend who is coming to visit you. Give information about your neighborhood. Use George's email as a model.

1 Choose a friend to write to.
2 Collect information about your neighborhood.
3 Find or draw images to illustrate your email.
4 Write the first version of your email. Use vocabulary from Unit 8.

LOOK!

Use a warm greeting expression to say hello to your reader.

Hi Mustafa!

End your email with a nice goodbye phrase. Be polite.

I'll write to you again soon!

6 Switch your email with a classmate and check their work. Use the checklist below.

◯ a warm greeting
◯ clear paragraphs: general description of your neighborhood, details about a specific place, closing paragraph
◯ a nice goodbye phrase
◯ defining relative clauses

YOUR DIGITAL PORTFOLIO

Edit your email. Then publish it. Upload it to the class portfolio for everyone to see!

REVIEW
UNITS 7 AND 8

VOCABULARY

1 **Put the letters in the correct order to make words for video channels and label the images.**

- abeuyt
- kicongo
- ~~mgaing~~
- hlthea nad finetss
- reewsvi
- iencesc dan thec
- xiunbngo
- vggerlo

1

gaming

2

....

3

....

4

....

5

....

6

....

7

....

8

....

2 **Complete the sentences with the phrases below.**

- eat out
- ~~go to a concert~~
- have a sleepover
- play in a band
- throw a party
- watch series

1 Derek has tickets for Maroon 5. I really want to ......go to a concert......!
2 Logan likes to .... with his parents. His favorite restaurant is The Duck.
3 I'm going to .... with all my cousins on Friday night. I need my pajamas!
4 Jane is going to .... this Saturday for her birthday.
5 It's a rainy day. I'm going to stay home and .... on TV.
6 Bel plays the guitar and sings very well. I guess she's going to ....!

3 **Choose the odd one out.**

1 border / visa / (reside)
2 passport / permanent resident / immigrant
3 reside / border / feel at home
4 feel at home / live abroad / visa

4 **Complete the sentences with the correct opposites of the words below.**

- agree
- ~~happy~~
- like
- kind
- patient
- possible

1 George is very ....unhappy..... His parents are going on vacation without him.
2 The children .... with our decision. They don't want to go and live in France.
3 This is ....: I can't be in two places at the same time.
4 Yuri is so .... He never thinks about other people.
5 My grandma was very .... after the operation. She wanted to go home.
6 Corinne and Josh clean the yard every week. They really .... doing it.

LANGUAGE IN CONTEXT

5 **Write affirmative sentences or questions using the prompts. Use *'d* if possible.**

1 I / would / love / see / a movie / on Saturday
I'd love to see a movie on Saturday.

2 she / would / like / eat / Japanese food?
....

3 he / would / like / be / in a video?
....

4 I / would / love / meet / your sister
....

6 **Complete the sentences with the correct present progressive form of the verbs in parentheses.**

1 She 's going .... to a concert next Sunday. (go)
2 .... Theo .... a sleepover at his friend's house on Saturday? (have)
3 Neil and Jenny .... out tonight with their friends. (eat/not)
4 Cassia .... a song from her new album on TV this evening. (play)
5 .... Bruno .... a surprise party for his parents on Thursday? (throw)
6 .... she .... to the theater with you? (go)

7 **Complete the definitions with *who* or *that*.**

1 **bike** (n) a vehicle ....that.... many children can use to go to school

2 **best friend** (n) a person .... is always there for you

3 **mall** (n) a place .... is full of customers, but they often don't buy anything

4 **chocolate** (n) the food .... you need to make you feel better when your best friend isn't around

8 **Write one sentence with a non-defining relative clause using the two sentences and *who* or *which*.**

1 Doris and Dan live in the country. They are happy children.
Doris and Dan, who live in the country, are happy children.

2 Pete fixed my computer. He lives next door.
....

3 The dog was making a lot of noise. It is now quiet.
....

4 The border separates the two countries. It is closed.
....

CHECK YOUR PROGRESS

I CAN...

- talk about video channels and free-time activities.
- use polite offers: *would like to / would love to.*
- talk about immigration.
- use defining and non-defining relative clauses.

LEARN TO LEARN

Opposites Using Prefixes

Prefixes change the meaning of words. Keep a record of them, their meanings, and some example words.

dis- (negation)
disagree (not agree)
dishonest (not honest)

GLOBAL CHANGER EXTRAS

READING 1

ACROSS THE CURRICULUM / LANGUAGE AND ARTS

A JAPANESE FESTIVAL

1 **Look at the title and the images. Discuss the questions with a partner.**

1 What can you see in the images?

2 What things do you think people do at *Tanabata*?

2 R.01 **Read and listen to the article. Were your ideas in Exercise 1 correct?**

Tanabata – The Star Festival

Do you know any beautiful love stories? Well, the story I want to tell you is a really beautiful Japanese love story called *Tanabata*. Originally a Chinese legend, *Tanabata* tells the love story of two stars. Orihime (the star Vega) made beautiful clothes for her father, the Sky King, but she was sad because she didn't have time to meet anyone. So her father organized a meeting with Hikoboshi (the star Altair), the boy who worked with cows. They fell in love immediately and got married. They were so in love that later Orihime stopped making clothes and Hikoboshi stopped taking care of his cows. Orihime's father was angry. He said they couldn't live together and he ordered them to live on different sides of the river (the Milky Way). Orihime was very sad, but her father loved her very much. When Orihime started working again, he let them meet once a year, on the seventh day of the seventh month. The first time they tried to meet, they couldn't cross the river, so some birds came and made a bridge for Orihime. The legend says that when the sky isn't clear, the birds cannot come and the two stars cannot meet. So Japanese people always wish for amazing weather on that day!

To remember the great love of Orihime and Hikoboshi, people in Japan celebrate Tanabata ("the evening of the seventh") every year on July 7. They write wishes on small strips of colored paper called *tanzaku* and hang them on bamboo branches. The decorated streets and lively parades, food stalls, and fireworks make Tanabata an exciting festival all over Japan.

3 **Read the article again and answer the questions.**

1 Why is *Tanabata* called the Star Festival?

Because it celebrates the love story of two stars.

2 How did Orihime and Hikoboshi first meet?

3 What happened after Orihime and Hikoboshi first met?

4 Why was Orihime's father angry?

5 Why do Japanese people want good weather for Tanabata?

6 Why does Tanabata happen on July 7?

4 **Describe a legend that you like to a partner. Think about these questions:**

- What is its origin?
- Is it connected to a local festival?
- When and where does the legend take place?
- Who are the main characters and what happens to each person?

THINK!

Is the legend of Tanabata similar to any legends in your country?

READING 2

AROUND THE WORLD

URBAN ART

1 **Look at the title and the images. Discuss the questions with a partner.**

1 What can you see in the images?
2 Where can you see the images?

2 R.02 **Read and listen to the article. Were your ideas in Exercise 1 correct?**

MEXICAN MURALISM

Are you on a short visit to Mexico City? Come and see some of the greatest works of street art in the world, especially murals. Muralism has a long history in Mexico – the Aztec people covered their buildings in paintings – and in the 1920s the government used murals to send messages to the Mexican people. Today, muralism is a form of popular urban art that doesn't always have a message but people love looking at it! Even the police are happy as long as the artists get permission from the property **owners**.

Thanks to social media, Mexican street art is now famous, and the work of talented artists is appearing all around the city. Going to 20 de Noviembre Avenue is easily the best experience. Take a walk along this main street early or late in the day to see rows of street art on the **shutters** of the closed shops. Sometimes the artists used themes from the stores in their art, like women's faces on cosmetic stores.

The areas of Roma and Condesa are full of murals too, and the Parque México has some beautiful and detailed works. A favorite is a mural of a boy on a deer, the sacred animal of the Aztecs.

The Roma district is also home to the Urban Art Show, a free street art exhibition that shows the work of about 20 street artists in a gallery. Some artists think that street art only has a place outside in the streets. Others say galleries help to protect and **promote** artists' work. What do you think?

3 **Read the article again and answer the questions.**

1 What is the origin of muralism in Mexico?
The Aztecs covered their buildings in paintings.
2 Which street has art on the outside of a lot of stores?
....
3 Which areas does the writer recommend for good street art?
....
4 What is the Urban Art Show?
....
5 Why do some artists disagree with the Urban Art Show?
....
6 Why do some artists agree with the Urban Art Show?
....

4 **Match the words to the example sentences.**

1 owners ....
2 promote ....
3 shutters ....
a Come to Joe's pizza!
b The store is open now.
c These are our books.

THINK!

Is street art a good or a bad thing? Why?

READING 3

ACROSS THE CURRICULUM / HISTORY, LANGUAGE, AND ARTS

DISAPPEARING LANGUAGES

1 Look at the title and the image. Discuss the questions with a partner.

1 How many languages are there in the world?
2 Where in the world do people speak Rapa Nui?

2 R.03 Read and listen to the article. Were your ideas in Exercise 1 correct?

RAPA NUI *an endangered language*

Do you know how many languages there are in the world? Over 7,000! Some languages still have thousands of speakers but other languages will soon disappear. In fact, 43% of all languages in the world are endangered. Is it important to save endangered languages? Some people say we show who we are through our language – we show our culture.

One of these endangered languages is Rapa Nui, the language people speak on the island of Rapa Nui in Polynesia in the Pacific Ocean. The island, also called Easter Island or Isla de Pascua, is a special territory of Chile, and it is famous for its huge statues called Moai.

For many years the island had its own culture and traditions, but gradually during the twentieth century, the Rapa Nui people had contact with the outside world. Their language changed with new words from Spanish, English, French, and Tahitian.

There are now between 800–1,000 speakers of Rapa Nui and half of all Rapa Nui speakers are over 40 years old. Up until the 1990s, many people on the island spoke and wrote only in Spanish, and classes at school were also in Spanish. To preserve the language, some children now learn Rapa Nui in elementary school and there are textbooks in Rapa Nui. Will studying the language in school help to stop the Rapa Nui language from disappearing? Only time will tell us that.

Language	Total number of speakers
1 English	1,268 billion
2 Mandarin Chinese	1,120 billion
3 Hindi	637 million
4 Spanish	539 million
5 French	278 million
6 Standard Arabic	275 million
7 Bengali	267 million
8 Russian	257 million
9 Portuguese	252 million
10 Indonesian	199 million

3 Read the article again and answer the questions.

1 How many languages are endangered in the world?
About 43% of all languages are endangered.
2 Which country does Rapa Nui belong to?
....
3 Why is the island famous?
....
4 How did the Rapa Nui language change during the last century?
....
5 How many people speak Rapa Nui now?
....
6 How are they trying to stop the language from disappearing?
....

4 Look at the chart and discuss the questions.

1 Which language has the most speakers in the world?
2 Is your main language on the list?

THINK!

Why do you think some languages are becoming endangered?

READING 4

AROUND THE WORLD

STREAMING SERVICES

1 Look at the title and the image. Discuss the questions with a partner.

1 What do you think this person is doing?

2 What type of program is he looking at?

2 R.04 Read and listen to the article. Were your ideas in Exercise 1 correct?

WATCH WHAT YOU LIKE, WHEN YOU LIKE!

Netflix, HBO, and other streaming services let you watch what you like, when you like over the Internet! But what's the difference between these services and regular TV?

FAN COMMUNITY

Streaming services use friends' recommendations and reviews to build a fan base on social media, and FOMO (Fear of missing out) drives many teens to watch shows.

WHICH SUBSCRIPTION?

That depends on where you are! Subscribe to a US streaming library and you get 100% content, but subscribe to the same streaming service from, say, Peru and you'll see 67% of the movies because of exclusivity and rights. Check out what you can see where you are!

BINGE WATCHING

Many TV **viewers** watch series in binges – **episode** after episode, **season** after season, and they don't move from the sofa for hours! In fact, 60% of all TV viewers said they watch two or more episodes of a show one after another during the week, and 29% said they finish a new season 24 hours after it comes out!

SPOILERS

People aren't watching the same show at the same time, so it's difficult to avoid spoilers. A **spoiler** nowadays can be about the whole series, so be careful! There are apps to block content on social media, or you can just ask your friends not to tell you!

3 Read the text again and answer the questions.

1 What are streaming services?

They let you watch what you like, when you like over the Internet.

2 Why can a subscription to the same streaming service be different in different countries?

....

3 What is binge watching?

....

4 How can you avoid spoilers?

....

4 Complete the sentences. Use the words in bold in the article.

1 This is the second ....season.... . I watched the first last year. It was amazing!

2 Each .... is 55 minutes, so I can easily watch three this evening.

3 Millions of .... watched the movie online in its first week.

4 Jade's brother posted a .... on his blog. His friends were mad!

THINK!

Which is better, regular TV or streaming?

PUZZLES & GAMES

UNIT 1

1 **Complete the crossword with the opposites of the words in bold. What's the opposite of the secret word?**

1 The historic center is **dull** and boring. Let's go somewhere more interesting!
2 Toni likes to listen to **lively** music when he's studying.
3 This beach is always **empty** on the weekend.
4 The village festival is very **traditional** – everyone cooks and dances in the street.
5 We're not going downtown. It's too **quiet**.

2 **Read the information in the chart and sentences a–e. Then complete the chart with the student's name.**

Name of Student	Name of School	Number of Students	Distance from Downtown	Age of School	After-school Activities
1 Joshua	Lapster School	1,230	250 m	15 years	music
2	Alterton School	850	900 m	3 years	robotics
3	Johnson School	600	100 m	25 years	music
4	Newford School	450	500 m	1 year	baseball club
5	Savanna School	1,750	300 m	6 years	programming

a No one goes to a school starting with the same letter as their name.
b Joshua and Lily both do music after school.
c Anna's school is smaller than Lily's school.
d Sam's school is farther from downtown than Anna's school.
e Noah's school is older than Sam's school.

UNIT 2

4 **Put the words with the same color in the correct order. Then write complete sentences.**

biggest · Earth · Tokyo · Deserts · planet · lake · farthest · Lake Baikal · world · Mercury · deepest · sun · sun · hottest · Neptune · city · planet · closest · places · world

1 Deserts are the hottest places on Earth.
2 ....
3 ....
4 ....
5 ....

3 **Complete sentences 1–11 and write the adjectives in the spiral crossword. Each adjective starts in the numbered square. Follow the spiral and write one letter in each square.**

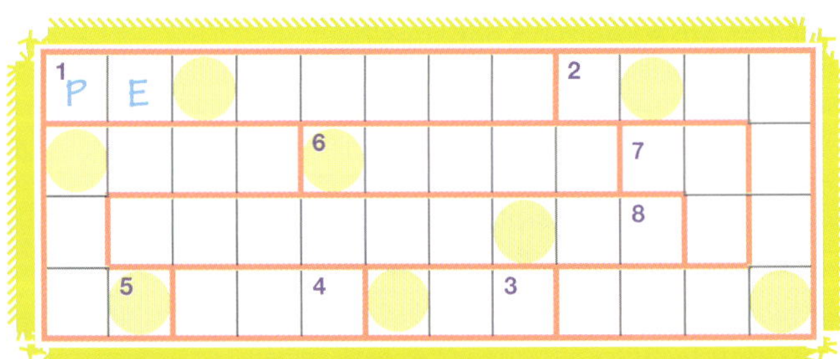

1 The lake near their hotel was p e a c e f u l and quiet.
2 Their i........ adventure started in the capital city.
3 It was good to have raincoats in the w........ weather.
4 There was d........ weather too, and it was a great place to watch animals.
5 They had a........ views from their hotel rooms.
6 They had an a........ vacation the year before.
7 They wanted to travel to a h........ country and go to the beach.
8 They had w........ food this time.

Where did they go to on vacation? Use the letters in the circles to make the name of a country in Africa.

....

UNIT 3

1 Look at the images and write the personality adjectives. Find and circle the words (→, ↓, ↘).

I	A	N	C	R	E	A	T	I	V	E
U	N	E	H	B	Q	W	L	S	C	A
O	X	D	E	S	E	R	I	O	U	S
I	I	A	E	J	D	U	W	C	V	Y
X	O	T	R	P	F	T	I	I	D	G
N	U	I	F	A	E	A	T	A	V	O
A	S	V	U	T	B	N	I	B	O	I
T	N	E	L	I	E	P	D	L	N	N
T	H	P	G	E	A	D	F	E	D	G
C	V	G	J	N	M	A	D	V	N	F
N	E	G	A	T	I	V	E	J	A	T

1  creative

2  ....

3  ....

4  ....

5  ....

6  ....

7  ....

8  ....

9  ....

10  ....

2 Match 1–5 with a–e.

1 

2 

3 

4 

5 

a Run quickly! You only have five minutes to catch the train. 5

b We worked fast and finished the job in only two days! ....

c So, can we check in immediately? ....

d The children are playing noisily in the yard again. It's making me so mad! ....

e He falls asleep very easily. He looks really peaceful! ....

UNIT 4

3 Match the photos with the phrases and complete the words to make money expressions.

1 

2 

3 

4 

5 

6 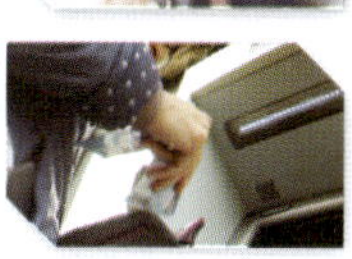

a b..........w money from your family

b s..........d spending money

c get b..........s from an A..........

d save c..........s

e use a d..........t c..........d to pay for things

f do jobs around the house and e..........n money

4 Put the words with the same color in order to make questions. Then answer the questions.

1 How ....

....

2 ....

....

3 ....

....

4 ....

....

UNIT 5

1 Look at the images and complete the crossword with the correct communication words.

Across

Down

2 Use the code and write the predictions about the future. Check (✓) the predictions you agree with.

1	2	3	4	5	6	7	8	9	10	11	12	13	14	15	16	17	18	19	20	21	22	23
D	E	C	W	I	A	U	T	S	O	K	F	M	R	V	H	L	N	Y	B	G	P	X

◯ 4 2   4 10 18 8   16 6 15 2   20 5 17 17 9   10 14   3 10 5 18 9.
W e ……

◯ 4 2   4 5 17 17   16 6 15 2   12 17 19 5 18 21   8 6 23 5 9.

◯ 22 2 10 22 17 2   4 5 17 17   16 6 15 2   14 10 20 10 8 9   6 8   16 10 13 2.

UNIT 6

3 Use the code to find the first and last letters of different occupations. Then write the words 1–7.

	1	2	3	4	5
A	a	b	c	d	e
B	f	g	h	i	j
C	k	l	m	n	o
D	p	q	r	s	t
E	u	v	w	x	y

1 A1 D3   a ...... r ......   actor
2 C3 C4 ....
3 C4 A5 ....
4 A3 B1 ....
5 D1 C4 ....
6 B4 D3 ....
7 A5 D3 ....

4 Start in the center of the spiral. Circle words to make four questions. Answer the questions for you.

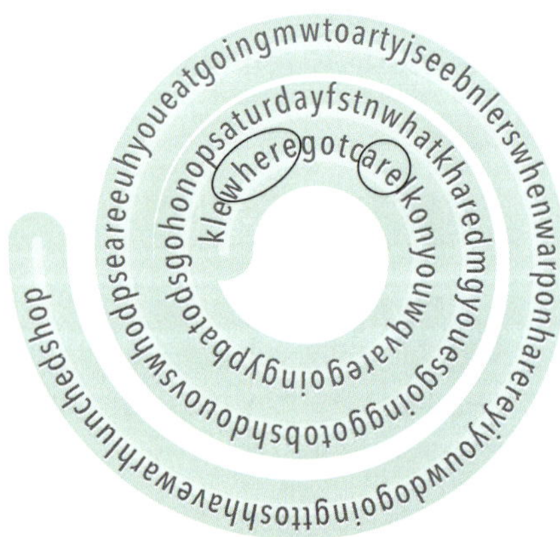

1 Q: Where are ....
A: ....
2 Q: ....
A: ....
3 Q: ....
A: ....
4 Q: ....
A: ....

UNIT 7

1 **Use the code to write the video channel words.**

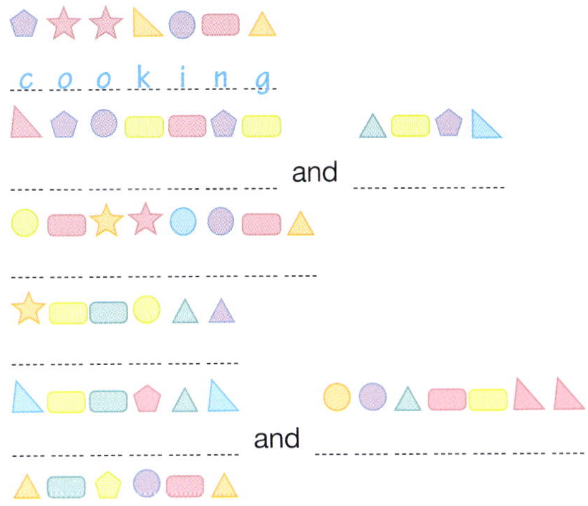

1 cooking

2 .... and ....

3 ....

4 ....

5 .... and ....

6 ....

2 **Read sentences 1–9 about what the people are doing on the weekend and write the names in the table. When isn't a person playing sports?**

	Saturday morning	Saturday afternoon	Sunday morning	Sunday afternoon
throw a party				Harry, Isabella
watch series				
play sports				

1 Harry and Isabella are having a birthday party on Sunday afternoon.
2 Rodrigo and Ana are watching series on Saturday afternoon.
3 Emma and Harry are playing basketball on Saturday morning and Isabella's playing on Saturday afternoon.
4 Ana's throwing a party on Saturday morning and Emma's having a party on Saturday afternoon.
5 Harry and Emma are both watching series on Sunday, but Harry in the morning and Emma in the afternoon.
6 On Saturday morning, Isabella's watching a series.
7 Rodrigo's throwing a party on Sunday morning and then in the afternoon he's playing football.

UNIT 8

3 **Use the letters of the same color and write seven words/phrases about living in another country. What secret word can you make with the letters in black?**

L	C	G	B	R	S	E	O	R	E
S	H	F	E	T	E	S	I	O	I
D	A	W	E	A	P	E	A	L	E
P	S	R	S	A	V	M	S	V	S
A	E	I	A	N	P	A	S	E	B
R	N	T	O	A	T	O	B	R	H
R	O	A	R	E	O	T	S	D	I
M	D	A	E	E	N	R	T	E	D

1 resides
2 c............
3 f............
4 l............
5 b............
6 g............
7 s............
secret word: i............

4 **Write one sentence using the sentences and *who* or *that*. Then match sentences 1–4 with images a–f.**

a

b

c

d

1 Amaya is a girl. She has a blue bag.
Amaya is the girl who has a blue bag. c
2 Sammy is a boy. He has the shortest hair.
.... ☐
3 Alessandro is wearing a shirt. It's green and blue.
.... ☐
4 Rita is a girl. She's wearing glasses.
.... ☐

PROJECT
DESCRIBING A GROUP OF PEOPLE

WRITE A FACT FILE ABOUT A GROUP OF PEOPLE WHERE YOU LIVE.

1 Look at the images on page 107. Discuss the questions with a partner.

1 What can you see?
2 What do you think the people are doing?
3 Where do you think the people live?

2 Read the fact file and complete the chart.

	The Bajau
Who and How Many?	*sea people*
Where?	
Lifestyle?	
How ... Different?	
Life Today?	

PROJECT TASK

1 PLAN

1 Choose a group of people where you live.
2 Find out about the people. Answer the questions in the chart in Exercise 2 for your group of people. Look for images.
3 Write your fact file using the information in your chart. Remember to include general information about the group of people, where they live, and what lifestyle they have. Is their lifestyle in danger?
4 Write and illustrate your fact file.
5 Check grammar, spelling and punctuation, and practice your pronunciation of any difficult words.
6 Record your fact file.

THINK!

Would you like to have the Bajau lifestyle? Does the fact file help you understand the lifestyle of a group of people? Why / Why not?

2 YOUR DIGITAL PORTFOLIO

Upload your fact file to the class portfolio for everyone to see! Present your fact file to the class.

3 REFLECT

Which is your favorite fact file? Why?

Impact | Our Programs | Our Explorers | Education Events | Funding Opportunities

The Bajau: Sea People

Who and Where?

The Bajau people live in Southeast Asia, in countries like the Philippines, Indonesia, and Malaysia. There are about one million Bajau people in the world. They typically live on boats called *lepas*, or in houses on or very near water.

Lifestyle

The Bajau are expert divers. They get everything from the ocean: their food and fish to sell. Their children learn to swim and hunt for fish at only eight years old. Bajau families use nets and spears to catch between one and eight kilos of fish a day. And the only thing they wear are wooden goggles!

How are they different?

The Bajau people aren't like any other humans on planet Earth. They can dive down 70 meters. Many Bajau can stay underwater for up to 13 minutes! How do they do that? They have spleens that are 50% bigger. The Bajau spleen gives the diver oxygen so they can stay underwater for longer. The Bajau also have incredible underwater vision to help them find fish and pearls.

Life Today

Life is changing for the Bajau. Many years ago the Bajau made their boats from light wood, but these trees are now endangered. Today, the new boats come from heavier wood, and this means they now need money to buy engines and fuel.

Fishing is also more difficult because the oceans are polluted. Many Bajau now live in houses in villages and they depend more on government help.

PROJECT

USING VISUALS TO SHOW INFORMATION

CREATE AN INFOGRAPHIC ABOUT IMMIGRATION WHERE YOU LIVE.

1 **Look at the infographic on page 109. What's the infographic about? Check (✓) the correct answer.**

- ◯ what people like to do in Australia
- ◯ people who go to live in Australia

2 **Read the infographic. What do these numbers refer to?**

a 190 *People from over 190 countries live and work in Australia.*
b 20 ....
c 250,000 ....
d 84% ....
e 34 ....
f one third ....

3 **Read the infographic again. Answer the questions.**

1 How many people live in Australia? *approximately 25,464,116*
2 What is the percentage of immigrant population? ....
3 Where do most immigrants come from nowadays? ....
4 Where do most immigrants live and work? ....
5 What's the average age of all immigrants? ....
6 How does immigration benefit Australia?
....
....

PROJECT TASK

1 **PLAN**

1 Find out about immigration where you live. Answer the questions in Exercise 3.
2 Look for images and information to use in the images.
3 Choose the images – maps, graphs, pie charts. Write the text. Remember to include information about where immigrants come from, where they live in your area, their average age, and how immigration benefits your area.
4 Design and create the infographic.
5 Check grammar, spelling and punctuation, and practice your pronunciation of any difficult words.

THINK!

Is the information about immigration in your country similar to or different from the infographic about Australia? Is immigration important in your country? Why?

2 **YOUR DIGITAL PORTFOLIO**

Upload your infographic to the class portfolio for everyone to see! Present your infographic to the class.

3 **REFLECT**

Which is your favorite infographic? Why?

Australian Immigration in Numbers

Australia is one of the most multicultural societies in the world, with people from over 190 countries living and working there. But what does immigration in Australia look like, and how does it benefit the country?

1. Total Population

25,464,116

is the approximate number of people living in Australia.

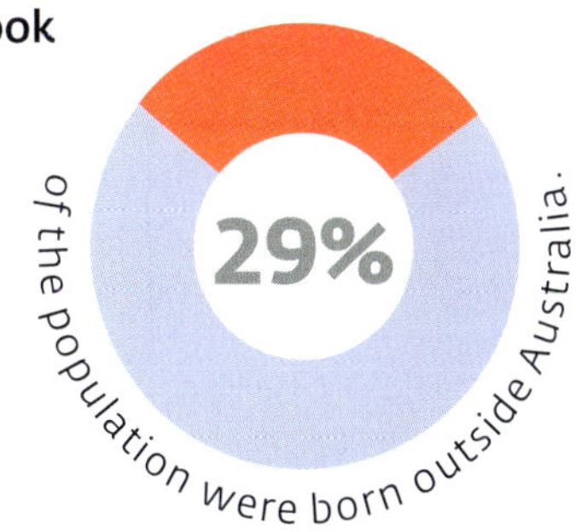

2. Where were they born?

20 years ago, immigrants in Australia were mainly from European countries, like the UK and Italy. Now, most immigrants come from China, India, and Malaysia. For example, there are 250,000 people from the Philippines living in Australia.

3. Where in Australia?

Most immigrants live and work in the biggest cities in Australia.

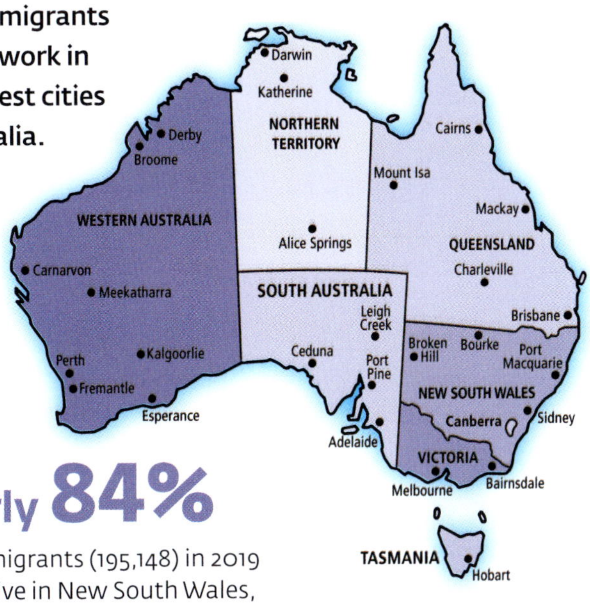

Nearly 84%

of all immigrants (195,148) in 2019 went to live in New South Wales, Victoria, and Queensland.

4. How old?

Australia's Population by Country of Birth

Country of Birth	Age
England	56
China	34
India	34
New Zealand	43
Philippines	40
Vietnam	46
South Africa	43
Italy	71
Malaysia	39
Scotland	59
All overseas-born	**44**

Australia has an aging population. New immigrants are usually much younger. The average age of all immigrants is 44, and Chinese and Indian immigrants have an average age of 34. This is better for the economy as they do not need healthcare or social services.

5. What are the benefits?

Immigrants own one third of the small businesses in Australia – **660,000** small businesses.

Immigrants pay **$80 billion** into the economy in taxes and also spend in their communities. Many send money home, so the country of origin also benefits.

Bringing their own language, traditions, and customs, immigrants make Australian culture more diverse and multicultural.

Immigrants help Australia grow, bringing new talent into many jobs. They are motivated, innovative, and entrepreneurial.

IRREGULAR VERBS

Infinitive	Simple Past
be	was / were
beat	beat
become	became
begin	began
break	broke
bring	brought
build	built
buy	bought
catch	caught
choose	chose
come	came
cost	cost
cut	cut
do	did
draw	drew
drink	drank
drive	drove
eat	ate
fall	fell
feel	felt
fight	fought
find	found
fly	flew

Infinitive	Simple Past
forget	forgot
get	got
give	gave
go	went
grow	grew
have	had
hear	heard
hide	hid
hit	hit
hold	held
keep	kept
know	knew
leave	left
lose	lost
make	made
meet	met
pay	paid
put	put
read	read
ride	rode
ring	rang
run	ran
say	said

Infinitive	Simple Past
see	saw
sell	sold
send	sent
show	showed
shut	shut
sing	sang
sit	sat
sleep	slept
speak	spoke
spend	spent
stand	stood
swim	swam
take	took
teach	taught
tell	told
think	thought
throw	threw
understand	understood
wake	woke
wear	wore
win	won
write	wrote

WORKBOOK CONTENTS

1 LIVE IT UP!

LANGUAGE REFERENCE

Comparatives: Short Adjectives

Most Adjectives	Adjectives Ending in *-y*	Adjectives Ending in Vowel + Consonant	Irregular Adjectives
close – clos**er**	angry – angr**ier**	big – bi**gger**	bad – **worse**
hard – hard**er**	easy – eas**ier**	hot – ho**tter**	good – **better**
long – long**er**	happy – happ**ier**	sad – sa**dder**	far – **farther**
nice – nice**r**	funny – funn**ier**	thin – thi**nner**	

Comparatives: Long Adjectives

Long Adjectives (2-syllable adjectives not ending in *-y* and all 3-syllable adjectives)
The food here is **more traditional than** the food in the other restaurant.
I think her paintings are **more unusual than** his.
She was **more surprised than** her friend was.

Comparatives: (*not*) *as* … *as*

The swimming pool was **as cold as** the sea.
I'm **not as excited as** I was yesterday.
The mall is**n't as crowded as** it was last Saturday.

Long and Short Adjectives 1

calm
crowded
dull
empty
exciting
lively
noisy
quiet
traditional
unusual

Festivals and Celebrations

atmosphere
crowds
dance show
fireworks
music event
souvenirs

VOCABULARY

1 Find nine adjectives.

po~~dull~~sorexcitingbritraditionaleaquietsyunusualzorurcalmcesponoisymarurlivelyghoempty

1 dull
2
3
4
5
6
7
8
9

2 Circle the correct options.

1 The cafeteria was so (*noisy*) / *quiet* / *calm* – I couldn't hear what Alex was saying.
2 There were a lot of people at the street market. It was very *calm* / *crowded* / *dull*.
3 The baby's sleeping. Please be *excited* / *lively* / *quiet*!
4 I didn't see anyone on my way to the park this morning. The streets were *lively* / *crowded* / *empty*.
5 There are no movie theaters or skateparks in that part of town. It's very *dull* / *lively* / *exciting*.
6 There's a lot of music here, and people are dancing in the streets. It's really *quiet* / *calm* / *lively*.

3 Look at the images and complete the words and phrases.

1

dance show

2

s..........

3

f..........

4

m.......... e..........

5

c..........

4 Match 1–6 with a–f.

1 I went to a really good dance b
2 A crowd of ....
3 The children like to buy souvenirs ....
4 We all enjoyed the music ....
5 The atmosphere at the soccer game ....
6 The fireworks in the evening ....

a 10,000 people watched the fireworks.
b show while I was in New York.
c was fantastic.
d events at the festival.
e when they're on vacation.
f were awesome!

GRAMMAR

1 Complete the sentences with the comparative forms of the adjectives in parentheses.

1. Your house is *bigger* (big) than mine.
2. The beaches are ______ (empty) than yesterday.
3. The weather is ______ (bad) than last week.
4. My headphones are ______ (good) than Daniel's.
5. Most people left an hour ago, so it's a lot ______ (calm) now.
6. The food here is ______ (nice) than the food in the Black Cat Café.

2 Put the words in the correct order.

1. think kayaking / I / more / than / is / interesting / fishing / .
   I think kayaking is more interesting than fishing.
2. me / was / more / Lara / surprised / than / .
   ______
3. than Madrid / more / is / Paris / expensive / .
   ______
4. was / excited / more / I / than / my mom / .
   ______
5. more / red dress is / the / beautiful / the black / than / dress / .
   ______
6. the / is / more / homework / math homework / difficult / than the English / .
   ______

3 Complete the sentences with the words below.

• ~~as~~ • as • as • isn't • isn't • wasn't

1. I wasn't as worried *as* my dad was.
2. I prefer Rome to London. London ______ as interesting as Rome.
3. The atmosphere at this year's festival wasn't ______ exciting as last year.
4. Let's go into the kitchen. The music there ______ as noisy as it is in here.
5. This dancing isn't as traditional ______ the dancing we saw yesterday.
6. Yesterday, the museum restaurant ______ as crowded as the café.

4 Complete the sentences with the correct comparative form of the adjective in parentheses.

1. You're *taller* than my brother. (tall)
2. The tickets for the game were ______ than the tickets for the show. (expensive)
3. It's definitely ______ today than it was yesterday. (hot)
4. This museum is ______ than the science museum! (dull)
5. The festival is ______ than last year. (crowded)
6. Love is ______ than money. (important)

READING

1 **Look at the text and check (✓) the correct answers.**

1 Who is the author?
- ◯ a blogger named Hannah
- ◯ a blogger named Tom

2 Look at the images. What do you think the blog post is about?
- ◯ an accident that happened when the writer was in Thailand
- ◯ an unusual festival in Thailand

HOME | ABOUT | BLOG CONTACT

TOM AND HANNAH'S TRAVELS

The Monkey Buffet

by Hannah Schorr

Readers of my blog know that I love going to unusual festivals around the world, but they may not know that I love monkeys. So, when I was in Thailand and I read about the Monkey Buffet festival in Lopburi, I really wanted to go!

If you don't know about this lively festival, here's what happens. One weekend in November, the people of Lopburi prepare an amazing banquet for the many (around 3,000!) macaque monkeys that live there. The food – about 4,000 kilograms of fruit, vegetables, rice, cakes, and candy – is put on long tables. Very soon, crowds of monkeys rush to the tables and start eating. It's a very popular festival – the monkeys attract a lot of tourists. There's also music and dancing and the atmosphere is fantastic.

Tom and I were in Thailand on the day of the festival, so we took the bus to Lopburi early in the morning. We had a really exciting day. It's awesome to watch all these monkeys sitting on tables and chairs, eating and drinking. One monkey near us was a bit bigger than the others – and obviously hungrier. He ate a pineapple, a pizza, and a dish of rice, and then took Tom's ice cream out of his hand and ate that, too!

Anyway, enjoy the photos. For travelers in Thailand in November, I really recommend the Monkey Buffet!

2 **Read the text and write *T* (true) or *F* (false) next to the statements.**

1 The writer read about the Monkey Buffet festival when she was in Thailand. T

2 The people of Lopburi make a lot of food for the tourists. ....

3 The monkeys eat only healthy food. ....

4 The festival is in December. ....

5 A lot of tourists come to watch the monkeys eat. ....

6 One monkey took Tom's ice cream. ....

3 **Write answers to the questions.**

1 What kind of events does the writer like going to?
She likes going to unusual festivals around the world.

2 How much food do the people of Lopburi prepare?
....

3 Where do they put the food?
....

4 How did Tom and Hannah travel to the festival?
....

5 What four things did the bigger monkey eat?
....

2 AMAZING PLACES

LANGUAGE REFERENCE

Superlatives: Short Adjectives

Short Adjectives			
Most Adjectives	**2-syllable Adjectives Ending in *–y***	**Adjectives with 1 Vowel and 1 Consonant**	**Irregular Adjectives**
brave – **the** brave**st** kind – **the** kind**est** long – **the** long**est**	happy – **the** happ**iest** lazy – **the** laz**iest** sunny – **the** sunn**iest**	big – **the** bi**ggest** hot – **the** ho**ttest** sad – **the** sa**ddest**	bad – **the worst** good – **the best** far – **the farthest**

We use superlatives to say that someone or something has more of a particular quality than all the other people or things in a group.

Superlatives: Long Adjectives

Long Adjectives (2-syllable adjectives not ending in –y and all 3-syllable adjectives)
This is **the most modern** part of the city center. This is **the most difficult** exercise of the three. It's **the most beautiful** city in the world. We had **the most amazing** food.

Long and Short Adjectives 2

amazing
awful
busy
cold
dry
hot
incredible
peaceful
terrible
wet
wonderful

Extreme Weather

blizzard
flood
forest fire
heatwave
hurricane
thunderstorm
tsunami

VOCABULARY

1 Find eight adjectives that describe places.

1 wonderful
2 ……
3 ……
4 ……
5 ……
6 ……
7 ……
8 ……

T	E	W	O	N	D	E	R	F	U	L
E	I	E	H	I	R	L	I	V	A	M
R	D	T	B	K	Y	I	A	U	W	P
R	E	B	U	S	Y	T	Y	I	F	O
I	C	Y	I	M	B	A	E	H	U	L
B	I	N	C	R	E	D	I	B	L	E
L	A	Z	I	P	C	T	E	Y	A	V
E	U	B	X	A	M	A	Z	I	N	G

2 Circle the correct options.

1

It was a really (hot) / *cold* / *wet* day.

2

It's so *dry* / *cold* / *wet*. We need some rain.

3

I love this place. It's so *peaceful* / *awful* / *busy*.

4

At this time of year, it's very *dry* / *hot* / *wet*.

5

It's really *hot* / *cold* / *wet* here.

3 Match words 1–7 with meanings a–g. Then match 1–7 with images A–G.

1 forest fire e D
2 flood …… ……
3 hurricane …… ……
4 blizzard …… ……
5 heatwave …… ……
6 thunderstorm …… ……
7 tsunami …… ……

a a very large wave
b a violent, circular wind
c when it's very hot for a few weeks
d too much water in a place
e a fire in an area of many trees
f when it's very snowy and windy
g rainy, windy weather with loud noises and bright lights in the sky

A

B

C

D

E

F

G

GRAMMAR

1 Write the superlative from of the adjectives.

1 dry the driest
2 big
3 happy
4 wet
5 small
6 windy
7 brave
8 sad

2 Complete the sentences with the correct superlative form of the adjectives below.

• bad • busy • ~~lazy~~ • small

1 My sister is the laziest person I know. She never helps at home.
2 These are the ______ souvenirs in the store. They're really awful.
3 It's the ______ city in Japan. The traffic never stops.
4 This is the ______ town in the UK. Only 381 people live there.

3 Complete the sentences with the superlative form of the adjective in parentheses. Then match sentences 1–4 with images a–d.

1 It's the most crowded city on Earth. (crowded) b
2 She was wearing ______ hat. (unusual) ______
3 Nathan cooked ______ meal. (incredible) ______
4 They were ______ sneakers in the store. (expensive) ______

a

b

c

d

4 Cross out the incorrect words and write the correct words below.

John
11:32 a.m.

We are having the ~~incredibliest~~ vacation. This is the beautifulest place. I love it. It has the most big area of forest in this part of the US, with the tallest trees in the world. (I think it has the oldest trees, too.) We walk for hours every day. Yesterday was the most hot day. We were so tired in the evening. I had the good sleep last night. See you all in a week.

like comment share

1 most incredible
2
3
4
5

READING

1 Look at the text and check (✓) the correct answers.

1 Who is now living in a different country?
- ◯ Aline
- ◯ Luisa
- ◯ Marcia

2 How does this person feel?
- ◯ Happy because she likes her new home and the place where she's now living.
- ◯ Sad because she isn't with her friends.

TODAY

Hi everyone!
Hope you're all good! We're doing well here. We like our new home. People say this is the most beautiful part of California. I don't know if that's true, but it's very nice! We're ten minutes from an incredible beach and we're also near a forest. We went to the beach yesterday evening, and we were the only people there. It was so peaceful. My brother's very excited about surfing 🏄. 8:11 ✓✓

Aline de Oliveira
Hey Luisa, good to hear from you! Pleased to hear you're happy there. California sounds amazing, especially the beach! How's your new home? 12:03

Great. It's on a hill and I can see the ocean from my bedroom window. It's a lot bigger than our Lisbon apartment 🙂! How is Lisbon without me 😉? Is it hot there? Today is the hottest day this week 😓. Last year, there was a heatwave here, and they had the worst forest fires in ten years. They were awful! I hope it isn't as hot this year … 12:22 ✓✓

Marcia Sylva
Yes, it's hot here too – and noisy. (Hi Luis!) We're sad without you here in Lisbon 😕. I'm thinking about that nice Californian beach … Speak soon, M xxx 12:25

2 Read the text and write *T* (true) or *F* (false) next to the statements.

1 Luisa now lives in a new home. T
2 She lives near the ocean. ....
3 Her home is in Lisbon. ....
4 The beach near Luisa was crowded last night. ....
5 Luisa's apartment in Lisbon was smaller than her new home. ....
6 There are forest fires now where Luisa lives. ....

3 Write answers to the questions.

1 Where does Luisa live now?
She lives in California.

2 What two things does she live near?
....

3 What is her brother excited about?
....

4 What can Luisa see from her bedroom window?
....

5 What happened in the forest near Luisa's new home last year?
....

3 THE ART OF EMOTIONS

LANGUAGE REFERENCE

Gerunds

Gerunds Before Verbs	Gerunds After Verbs
Swimming is great. **Waiting** for the bus is really boring. **Painting** is fun.	He loves **riding** his bike. I like **drawing** the birds in the backyard. We enjoy **swimming** in the sea.

Adverbs of Manner

Regular	
Adjectives	**Adverbs**
She was very **serious** when she spoke. He's a **beautiful** singer. We were very **anxious** at the hospital.	She spoke very **seriously**. He sings **beautifully**. We waited **anxiously** at the hospital.

Irregular		
Adjectives/Adverbs	**Adjectives**	**Adverbs**
good/well	She's a very **good** painter.	She paints very **well**.
fast/fast	He's a **fast** runner.	He can run **fast**.
hard/hard	This is **hard** work.	They work **hard**.

Personality Adjectives

anxious
cheerful
creative
easygoing
independent
mad
negative
patient
serious
sociable

Art

artist
collages
drawing
graffiti
mural
stencils
stickers
technique

VOCABULARY

1 Circle the correct options.

1 Eva's never sad or serious. She's very *cheerful* / *negative* / *anxious*.
2 Sam's very *creative* / *anxious* / *sociable*. He loves hanging out with his friends.
3 My brother never expects good things. He's very *negative* / *cheerful* / *patient*.
4 My cousin is very *easygoing* / *independent* / *serious*. He doesn't need my help.
5 She's a very *patient* / *anxious* / *negative* teacher. She's really calm and never gets angry.
6 My cousin is a really good artist. He's very *negative* / *creative* / *anxious*.

2 Match 1–6 with a–f.

1 Sarah's extremely serious. d
2 Naomi's very cheerful. ....
3 Amy's very creative. ....
4 Rebecca's an anxious person. ....
5 Millie's very easygoing. ....
6 Sophie's mad at me. ....

a She's really angry.
b She makes friends easily.
c She often has new ideas.
d She's not really a funny person.
e She's often worried about something.
f She's always happy.

3 Label images 1–6 with the words below.

• collages • ~~drawing~~ • graffiti • mural • stencils • stickers

1 
drawing

2 
....

3 

....

4 
....

5 
....

6 
....

4 Put the letters in the correct order and write the words for the definitions.

1 pictures made with different materials, or made with different pictures collages (glosalce)
2 method of doing something .... (quinhetce)
3 large painting on a wall .... (lurma)
4 picture made with a pencil or pen .... (gawndir)
5 words or drawings on walls, doors, etc. in public places .... (ifigtarf)
6 someone who makes drawings, paintings, etc. .... (ritsta)

GRAMMAR

1 Complete the sentences with the gerund form of the verbs in parentheses.

1 ....Going.......... to bed early is boring. (go)
2 He doesn't like .... fried food. (eat)
3 My friend and I love .... things. (invent)
4 .... photos with my new camera is really easy. (take)
5 .... languages is really interesting. (learn)
6 I especially like .... pictures of people. (paint)

2 Make sentences with the prompts using the simple present and the gerund form.

1 get up / early / very difficult
Getting up early is very difficult.
2 Jake / love / play volleyball
....
3 make dinner / with my friends / fun
....
4 My sister and I / like / dance
....
5 She / not like / do exercise
....
6 sit down / all day / not healthy
....

3 Are the underlined words adjectives or adverbs? Circle *adj.* (adjective) or *adv.* (adverb).

1 Ella draws very well. *adj.* / *adv.*
2 Our teacher speaks very quickly. *adj.* / *adv.*
3 Dan's very patient with his little brother. *adj.* / *adv.*
4 My aunt's a very fast runner. *adj.* / *adv.*
5 The exercises were very easy. *adj.* / *adv.*
6 That's a very good painting. *adj.* / *adv.*

4 Complete the sentences with the adverb form of the adjectives in parentheses.

1 He spoke very ....seriously.... about the problem. (serious)
2 She swims very .... for a six-year-old. (good)
3 My parents both work really .... (hard)
4 My uncle drives very .... (fast)
5 The boys ate their dinner very .... (noisy)
6 She looked out the window .... (anxious)

READING

1 Read the text quickly and check (✓) the correct answers.

1 What shows that the text is from an official website?
- ◯ the titles
- ◯ the menu
- ◯ the images

2 What is the objective of the text?
- ◯ to tell people how to paint
- ◯ to persuade people to talk to each other
- ◯ to persuade people to take the classes

HOME | PICTURE GALLERY | OUR TUTORS | CONTACT PAGE

CALM ART

Introduction to the Classes

We all feel anxious and sad some of the time. It's natural. Many people can talk about their emotions, but for some people, expressing emotions with words is difficult. For these people, it's easier to express those feelings through painting and drawing. They can tell everyone how they feel by the pictures that they create, or the colors that they use.

At Calm Art, we believe that creating art is good for people. For two hours in the evening, our students concentrate on making one piece of art – and nothing else. They paint or draw, and those negative feelings disappear.

Some of our students find they work creatively in our studio. Others prefer to paint in our beautiful, peaceful garden. Our friendly, qualified teachers are here to help.

We have all the materials you need for painting, drawing, making collages, or working with stencils. Everything you need is here.

What our students say:

"After a long day working in a noisy classroom, I love coming to Calm Art. It really helps me to relax. Friendly teachers and an awesome, modern studio. I recommend it."

Sophia

"As a child, I was very creative and loved making things with my hands. Then, I got older and stopped creating art. At Calm Art, I'm making beautiful things again and I love it!"

Lucas

2 Read the text and check (✓) the word/phrase that completes each sentence.

1 Calm Art helps people to …
- ◯ paint better pictures.
- ✓ express their emotions.
- ◯ meet other students.

2 For two hours, students …
- ◯ create a piece of art.
- ◯ talk about their work.
- ◯ talk about their feelings.

3 Students work in a …
- ◯ garden.
- ◯ studio.
- ◯ garden or studio.

4 Sophia likes the …
- ◯ garden.
- ◯ materials.
- ◯ teachers and studio.

5 Lucas …
- a ◯ didn't like art at school.
- b ◯ liked art when he was young.
- c ◯ started doing art at 25.

3 Write answers to the questions.

1 What is difficult for some people?
expressing emotions with words

2 What happens to negative feelings when students paint or draw?
....

3 As well as painting and drawing, which other art techniques can students use?
....

4 Where does Sophia work during the day?
....

4 LIFESTYLES

LANGUAGE REFERENCE

Countable and Uncountable Nouns

	Countable	Uncountable
Nouns	a hamburger, an egg, a hat, a jacket, an idea	cheese, rice, water, exercise
Affirmative (+)	I ate **a burger** and **an egg**. She had **some** cool **hats**. 	We had **some cheese**. There was **some rice**. 
Negative (–)	There weren't **any jackets**.	There wasn't **any water**.
Questions (?)	Did he have **any ideas**?	Did you do **any exercise**?

Countable nouns are things we can count. Uncountable nouns are things we can't count. Some countable nouns are always plural, for example *pants*, *shorts*.

Quantifiers

Countable: *How many ...?* *a lot of ... / (not) many*	Uncountable: *How much ...?* *a lot of ... / (not) much*
How many bikes do you have? I have **a lot of** T-shirts. There are **many** movie theaters in town. I do**n't** have **many** coats.	**How much** food is there? There's **a lot of** rice. There is**n't much** pasta. I do**n't** eat **much** chocolate.

To ask questions about quantities we use *How many* with countable nouns. We use *How much* with uncountable nouns. We use *many* (not *a lot of*) in more formal affirmative sentences.

Shopping 1

ATM
bills
borrow
coins
debit card
earn
money
save
spend
spending money

Shopping 2

afford
bargain
customer
donate
free
price
sales associate
shopping center

VOCABULARY

1 Match 1–6 with a–f.

1 money ....c....
2 debit card ....
3 coins ....
4 spending money ....
5 ATM ....
6 bills ....

a

b

c

d

e

f

2 Circle the correct options.

1 I (save) / *borrow* some of my spending money every week. I now have over $100.
2 I need some money to buy a coffee. Can I *spend* / *borrow* three dollars from you, please?
3 Did you get these *bills* / *coins* from the ATM?
4 I *earn* / *save* some money by cleaning my uncle's car.
5 Every week, I *borrow* / *spend* five or six dollars on drinks and candy.
6 I'm waiting for the bank to send me my new *spending money* / *debit card*.

3 Find seven shopping words.

rab~~bargain~~profreeverbdonatebrolcustomercarstsalesassociateumtaffordlopwerprice

1 ....bargain....
2 ....
3 ....
4 ....
5 ....
6 ....
7 ....

4 Complete the sentences with the words below.

• afford • bargain • ~~free~~ • price • sales associate • shopping center

1 You don't need money for the lemonade. It's ....free.....
2 I gave the .... the money for the bread.
3 There are a lot of clothes stores in the ....
4 My jeans were only $20. They were a ....!
5 These shoes are too expensive. I can't .... them.
6 How much is this hat? I can't see a .... on it.

GRAMMAR

1 Complete the chart with the words below.

- ~~artist~~ • book • chair • hotel • ketchup • keyboard
- lake • milk • pineapple juice • rice • salt • taxi

Countable Nouns	Uncountable Nouns

artist	....
....	....

2 Circle the correct options.

1 There *were* / *weren't* some street markets.
2 I need *an* / *some* information about the school.
3 There *weren't* / *wasn't* any milk on the table.
4 They didn't have *any* / *some* pizza on the menu.
5 I need to save *some* / *any* money for my vacation.
6 We didn't see *some* / *any* birds there.

3 Complete the questions with *how many* or *how much*.

1 ......How many...... bedrooms are in your house?
2 .... soup is there?
3 .... debit cards do you have?
4 .... work did you do today?
5 .... sugar do you have in your coffee?
6 .... movie theaters are there in your town?

4 Complete the dialogue with the words/phrases below.

- ~~a lot of~~ • a lot of • how many • how much • many • much • some

Camila That's a new T-shirt, isn't it, Victor? You have [1] ......a lot of...... clothes! [2] ......How much...... do you spend on them?

Samuel I don't know – about forty dollars a month.

Camila Forty dollars! That's [3] .... money! What clothes do you like to buy most?

Samuel Hmm … T-shirts. I really like T-shirts.

Camila [4] .... T-shirts do you have?

Samuel About twenty.

Camila Wow! I don't have [5] .... T-shirts – only three or four. I don't like to spend [6] .... money on clothes, but I love ice cream. Let's get [7] .... ice cream now!

READING

1 Read the text quickly and check (✓) the correct answers.

1 What is the objective of the blog?
- ◯ to inform people about new styles of clothes
- ◯ to persuade people not to buy new clothes

2 The author thinks secondhand clothes ...
- ◯ often have better quality.
- ◯ are better for the planet.

You are here: Home | About | Contact

Other People's Clothes!

Other People's Clothes

Hi and welcome to *Other People's Clothes!*

I'm Patricia and I live in São Paulo with my parents and younger sister. I started writing this blog six months ago because I want to encourage my friends to buy secondhand clothes. I really love clothes, but I don't have much money so I can't afford to buy new clothes from the clothes store. (I get $15 spending money a week, and a little extra that I earn by washing my parents' car – that's all.) So, here's what I do – I buy secondhand clothes online. You can find some real bargains. Last week, for example, I bought some jeans for $15. They're perfect. In the store, these jeans cost $70. How cool is that!

Here's another reason not to buy new clothes. There are so many clothes in the world now. We need to wear the clothes that already exist, not make even more clothes! Let's recycle clothes! Companies only make new clothes because we buy them. Stop buying them and they will stop making them!

OK, the online photographs of the clothes sometimes look better than the clothes when they arrive! This only happened to me once, with a jacket. I donated it to a charity store. Next time you want a new T-shirt or sweater, go online and look at all the secondhand clothes you can buy! Oh – and please post a photo of your amazing new (old) clothes below!

2 Read the text and circle the correct options.

1 Patricia lives with her *friends* / *family*.
2 Patricia wants her friends to buy *new* / *old* clothes.
3 Last week, she spent *$70* / *$15* on some jeans.
4 She wants companies to *stop making* / *make* more new clothes.
5 The online photographs sometimes look *worse* / *better* than the clothes when they arrive.
6 She once bought a *T-shirt* / *jacket* online that she didn't like.

3 Write *T* (true) or *F* (false) next to the statements.

1 Patricia started writing the blog six months ago. ....
2 She buys a lot of new clothes. ....
3 She wants her friends to buy more new clothes. ....
4 She is worried about all the clothes that exist in the world. ....
5 She often gives the clothes she buys online to charity stores. ....
6 She wants to see pictures of her friends' secondhand clothes. ....

5 LET'S TALK.

LANGUAGE REFERENCE

Simple Future

Affirmative (+)	Negative (–)	Questions (?)
I **will travel** to Europe. You **will be** a famous artist one day. He/She **will be** at home tonight. We **will take** public transportation more. They **will call** us at eight o'clock.	I **won't travel** by boat. You **won't be** a teacher one day. He/She **won't be** at the party tonight. We **won't drive** our cars as much. They **won't send** us a message first.	**Will** we **live** in smaller houses in a hundred years? **Will** we **be** happier in the future?

We use will (*'ll*) or will not (*won't*) to say what we think will or will not happen in the future.

Future with *be going to*: Affirmative

I**'m going to** call Adriana this evening.
You**'re going to** meet Marcia tonight.
He/She**'s going to** donate some clothes.
We**'re going to** drive to the airport.
They**'re going to** fly to Mexico.

We use *be going to* to talk about things that we intend to do in the future.

Communication 1

call
communicate
emojis
face-to-face
language
message
text
video chat
virtual communication

Communication 2

debate
describe
explain
say
speak
tell
translate

VOCABULARY

1 Look at images a–f and complete the sentences with the correct communication words. Then match 1–6 with a–f.

1 Olivia and I met f*ace* -t*o* -f*ace* in the office. *d*
2 I got a text m.................... from Fernanda last night. ....
3 He had a phone c.................... from his sister yesterday. ....
4 She uses a lot of e.................... in her messages. ....
5 I can't meet you tomorrow, but we could have a v.................... c..................... ....
6 Speaking to people is very nice, but it's sometimes more convenient to t..................... ....

a

b

c

d

e

f

2 Match the words with the definitions.

1 text *e*
2 communicate ....
3 language ....
4 face-to-face ....
5 virtual communication ....
6 emoji ....

a being in the same place as another person that you are meeting
b speak or write to someone
c small image, often a face, that shows an idea or feeling
d system of communication, for example, Spanish
e use a phone to send written messages
f speaking or writing using a computer or other electronic device

3 Match 1–6 with a–f.

1 She described her brother *b*
2 Maria said ....
3 My grandmother spoke ....
4 I translated the Portuguese ....
5 My brother told ....
6 The teacher explained ....

a the party was wonderful.
b as tall, with dark hair.
c me he was anxious.
d how to do the exercise.
e four languages.
f into English.

4 Put the letters in the correct order and complete the sentences.

1 She wants to *translate* (snatrtale) the book into French.
2 They plan to .... (bedeta) the problem tomorrow.
3 Could you .... (esdiberc) the painting to me?
4 Please can you .... (pliexan) how to use this printer?
5 Do you .... (kapes) Italian?
6 .... (lelt) me about your vacation.

GRAMMAR

1 Complete the sentences with *will* (+) or *won't* (–) and the verbs below.

• do • ~~drive~~ • eat (x 2) • go • pay

1 We *won't drive* (–) cars in the future.
2 Children .... (–) to school in future.
3 We .... (+) more fruit and vegetables in the future.
4 Maybe we .... (–) any meat.
5 We .... (–) for things with money.
6 People .... (+) more exercise at home.

2 Put the words in the correct order to make questions.

1 future / wear / in the / will / different / we / clothes / ?
Will we wear different clothes in the future?
2 will / the future / our houses / be different / in / ?
....
3 planet / will / our / be / in fifty / hotter / years / ?
....
4 in / use / will / we / years / phones / twenty / ?
....
5 all speak / we / the / will / language / same / ?
....

3 Match 1–6 with a–f to make six phrases. Then look at images A–F and complete the sentences with the correct form of be going to and the phrases.

1 have *b*
2 do ....
3 go ....
4 read ....
5 cook ....
6 take ....

a some chicken
b a video chat
c his homework
d some photos
e a book
f sightseeing

This afternoon, …

A

They *'re going to have a video chat*.

B

She ....

C

He ....

D

I ....

E

She ....

F

We ....

READING

1 Read the text quickly and check (✓) the correct answers.

1 What does the author predict for the future?
- ◯ Animals will speak like people.
- ◯ We will understand what animals are saying.

2 How will this help us?
- ◯ We will chat with animals.
- ◯ We will give better treatment when animals are sick.

What did that horse say?

BY LUCAS WALKER

We already know that animals communicate with other animals and people. They say hello by making noises and moving parts of their bodies. For example, when two horses meet, they put their noses together. Chimpanzees touch hands to say hello. They also put their arms up to tell other chimpanzees that there is danger. Animals say a lot of other things too, but we don't understand their language.

However, some scientists hope that one day in the future, we will understand what animals are saying. And, even more exciting, we will communicate with them!

So how will this happen? Well, scientists are collecting thousands of videos, for example, of dogs' noises and facial expressions. They will use artificial intelligence to learn how to translate these noises and expressions into a language that humans can understand. We will discover the emotions that animals are expressing and the messages that they are trying to give us.

Of course, this will be fascinating, but will it help us in any way? Well, yes! We will know if our pets are sick, and we will know which part of their body is hurting. This means we will be able to treat them more successfully. It also means we will get to know our pets better. And that's a very good thing!

2 Read the text and complete each sentence with one word.

1 Animals speak to each other by moving parts of their bodies and making *noises*.
2 Horses use their .... to say hello to other horses.
3 Chimpanzees use their .... to say hi to other chimpanzees.
4 Scientists want to .... animal noises and expressions into a language that we can understand.
5 We will know if they are .... and can try to make them better.

3 Write answers to the questions.

1 How do animals say hello?
They make noises and move parts of their bodies.

2 Why do chimpanzees put their arms up?
....

3 What are scientists collecting?
....

4 What type of intelligence will scientists use?
....

5 We will treat our pets more successfully, what other things will we probably do?
....

6 EXTRAORDINARY LIVES

LANGUAGE REFERENCE

Future with *be going to*

Affirmative (+)	Negative (–)	*Yes*/No Questions (?)	Short Answers
I'**m going to** have a video chat with Francisco this evening. We'**re going to** donate some clothes to a charity store.	I'**m not going to** spend this money. He'**s not going to** invite Lucas to the party.	**Is** it **going to** rain today? **Are** they **going to** explain what happened?	Yes, it **is**./No, it'**s not**. Yes, they **are**./No, they'**re not**.

Wh– Questions (?)
What **are** you **going to** tell Aline? When **is** she **going to** see Luis?

We use *be going to* to talk about things that we intend to do in the future.

Intensifiers

Countable Nouns: *too many, (not) enough*	Uncountable Nouns: *too much, (not) enough*
There are **too many** jackets in the closet. There are **enough** bargains for everyone. There are **not enough** flowers in this yard. There are**n't enough** chairs in the dining room.	There's **too much** cheese on the pizza. There's **enough** salt in the food already. There's **not enough** butter on this bread. There is**n't enough** milk in my coffee.

Occupations

actor
athlete
chef
dancer
engineer
fashion designer
inventor
musician
nurse
politician
writer

Adjectives to Describe People

available
flexible
helpful
reliable
successful
suitable

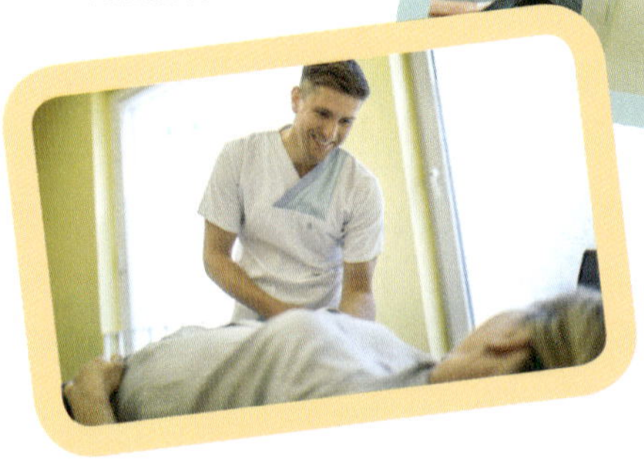

VOCABULARY

1 Match 1–6 with a–f.

1 nurse ....c....
2 politician ....
3 engineer ....
4 chef ....
5 musician ....
6 fashion designer ....

a

b

c

d

e

f

2 Put the letters in the correct order to make occupations.

1 This person creates paintings, drawings, etc.
sitrat ......artist......
2 This person creates stories.
retriw ....
3 This person moves their body to music.
naderc ....
4 This person is in movies and plays.
catro ....
5 This person can run, jump, and throw things well.
eettlah ....
6 This person designs and makes new things.
ronevint ....

3 Find six adjectives to describe people.

ahouth~~helpful~~raabreliablepixtrflexiblemobisuitableklirpexeuxsuccessfulveravailablerev

1 ......helpful......
2 ....
3 ....
4 ....
5 ....
6 ....

4 Circle the correct options.

1 Is the movie *reliable* / *suitable* for young children?
2 He's in a lot of movies. He's a very *successful* / *helpful* actor.
3 The principal was very *helpful* / *suitable* and gave me a map of my new school.
4 My grandma is a very *flexible* / *available* person. She listens to our new ideas.
5 Lucas always does what he says he will do. He's very *successful* / *reliable*.
6 Our math homework is very difficult. Are you *available* / *successful* to help us this afternoon?

GRAMMAR

1 Complete each sentence with one word.

1 ___What___ are you going to do this afternoon?
2 We're not ______ to drive to the beach.
3 ______ they going to make pizza tonight?
4 When ______ Sophie going to call us?
5 He's not going ______ come on vacation with us.
6 I'm tired. I'm ______ going to go out this evening.

2 Put the words in the correct order to make questions and statements.

1 a picture / of the / paint / to / I'm / going / lake / .
I'm going to paint a picture of the lake.
2 going / you / Daniel / to / are / call / ?
______
3 not / ultra-processed food / going / we're / to / eat / .
______
4 going / to / early / go to / bed / I'm / .
______
5 call / are / going / you / to / your mom / ?
______
6 not / any money / to / he's / going / borrow / .
______

3 Check (✓) the two phrases that complete each sentence.

1 There are too many …
- ✓ pens in my bag.
- ✓ shoes in the closet.
- ○ sugar in my drink.

2 There's too much …
- ○ tables in this room.
- ○ water in my drink.
- ○ milk in this coffee.

3 There were too many …
- ○ food.
- ○ children in the gym.
- ○ cookies on the plate.

4 There was too much …
- ○ homework.
- ○ animals in the zoo.
- ○ butter on my bread.

5 There are too many …
- ○ cafés on this street.
- ○ glasses on the table.
- ○ soda in this glass.

6 There is too much …
- ○ bread for two people.
- ○ burgers for me.
- ○ meat on my plate.

4 Complete the sentences with the words below.

• aren't • enough • many • much • ~~there's~~ • too

1 ___There's___ too much ketchup on my burger!
2 There ______ enough people to play basketball.
3 There are too ______ clothes in your bag.
4 There's not ______ salt in this soup.
5 There's too ______ rice in this pan.
6 There are ______ many cars on the road.

READING

1 Look at the text and check (✓) the correct answers.

1 Who is the author of the text?
- ◯ the principal of the school
- ◯ the principal and the students at the school

2 What do the students write about?
- ◯ their plans for the future
- ◯ their experience of the school

Saying Goodbye ...

The principal writes:

At this time of year, we say goodbye to our wonderful students. We are sad to see them go, but excited about their plans for the future. Here, we talk to Mariana, Gabriel, and Amanda about what they're going to do next. All were fantastic students and I know they will have exceptional careers.

Mariana Did you know that only 20% of engineers are women? It's not enough, but I'm confident that it will change in the next ten years. I'm going to study engineering at a university in São Paulo. Five of my female friends are also going to study engineering. I think it's a suitable job for me because I'm good at math and science, and I work hard.

Gabriel I'm going to study fashion for three years in college, also in São Paulo, but before I do that, I'm going to work for a small company that makes clothes. It's important to get some experience before you study fashion. And why is this a suitable career for me? Well, obviously, I love clothes! I'm also very creative and I love working with my hands.

Amanda I'm going to study English (my favorite subject) in college. I'm really excited about it. One day, I want to be an English teacher. My friends tell me I'm helpful and reliable. I think those are good qualities for a teacher!

2 Read the text and questions (1–6). Check (✓) the correct person in the chart.

	Gabriel	Mariana	Amanda
1 Who's going to work before they go to college?	◯	◯	◯
2 Who says she works hard?	◯	◯	◯
3 Who wants to teach the subject she's going to study?	◯	◯	◯
4 Who enjoys using his/her hands to do things?	◯	◯	◯
5 Who has friends who are going to study the same subject?	◯	◯	◯

3 Answer the questions.

1 How does the principal feel about these students leaving school?
She's sad to say goodbye to them, but she's excited about the students' plans for the future.

2 According to Mariana, what percentage (%) of engineers are men?

....

3 Why does Mariana think she will be a good engineer?

....

4 How long is Gabriel going to be in college?

....

5 How do Amanda's friends describe her?

....

7 THIS IS FUN!

LANGUAGE REFERENCE

Polite Offers: *'d like to/'d love to/Would (you) like to ...?*

Affirmative (+)	*Yes/No* Questions (?)	Short Answers
I'**d like to** show you my paintings. You'**d love to** have a video chat with her. We'**d love to** visit them.	**Would** you **like to** see my paintings? **Would** you **like to** have a video chat tomorrow? **Would** we **like to** visit them on Friday?	Yes, I'**d love** to. / No, thank you. Yes, we'**d like** to. / No, thank you. Yes, we **would**. / No, we **wouldn't**.

***'d* is short for *would.* Note that we don't use *would ... love* in *Yes/No* questions.**

Present Progressive for Future Plans, Appointments, and Arrangements

Affirmative (+)	Negative (–)
I'**m going shopping** this afternoon. You'**re eating** out this evening. He'**s**/She'**s having** a sleepover tonight. We'**re playing** in a band tomorrow. They'**re going** to a concert on the weekend.	I'**m not going** out tonight. You'**re not seeing** anyone today. He/She'**s not watching** the baseball game today. We'**re not visiting** your parents this weekend. They'**re not having** a vacation this summer.
***Yes*/No Questions (?)**	**Short Answers**
Am I **seeing** you tomorrow? **Are** you **making** dinner this evening? **Is** he/she **coming** to the movie theater tonight? **Are** we **going** to Bruna's house this weekend? **Are** they **flying** to Mexico?	Yes, I **am**. / No, I'**m not**. Yes, you **are**. / No, you'**re not**. Yes, he/she **is**. / No, he/she'**s not**. Yes, we **are**. / No, we'**re not**. Yes, they **are**. / No, they'**re not**.

We also use the present progressive to talk about the planned future. Use time expressions that indicate future (*this afternoon*, *tonight*, *tomorrow*, *this weekend*, etc.).

Video Channels

beauty
cooking
gaming
health and fitness
reviews
science and tech
unboxing
vlogger

Free-time Activities

eat out
go to a concert
have a sleepover
play in a band
throw a party
watch series

VOCABULARY

1 Put the letters in the correct order to make different types of video channels. Then match 1–6 with a–f.

1 maggni ___gaming___ ___b___
2 verswie ______ ______
3 kinogoc ______ ______
4 ebatuy ______ ______
5 thehal and tifsens ______ ______
6 ciseenc and ceth ______ ______

a Luis likes learning how to prepare different types of food.
b Juliana uses the Internet to play with her friends.
c Marcos is interested in learning new exercises to stay strong.
d Aline listens to people's opinions on movies and TV programs.
e Patricia likes learning about new inventions and discoveries.
f Ana likes learning about new cosmetics.

2 Complete the text with the words below.

• beauty • cooking • ~~health and fitness~~ • reviews • unboxing • vlogger

My sister and I have very different interests, so we watch different videos. She's an athlete, so she watches the [1] ___health and fitness___ channels. She also loves new technology, so she watches people take new cell phones out of their boxes on the [2] ______ channels. I'm not really interested in any of that, but I love seeing all the new cosmetics, so I sometimes watch the [3] ______ channels. I especially like videos by Nikki – she's my favorite [4] ______. I also like hearing about new movies, so I sometimes watch the [5] ______ channels. And finally, to get ideas about what to make for dinner, I watch the [6] ______ channels.

3 Complete the sentences with one word.

1 Joe would like to ___play___ in a band – he'd love to learn the trumpet.
2 We're going to eat ______ tonight at my favorite restaurant.
3 Would you like to ______ to a concert?
4 Let's ______ a sleepover at my house on the weekend!
5 My sister is 18 next month and we're going to ______ a party for her.
6 I'd like to ______ series with you.

4 Look at the images. What are the free-time activities? Write phrases from Exercise 3.

1

___go to a concert___

2

______

3

______

4

______

5

______

6

______

GRAMMAR

1 Complete sentences 1–6 with *'d like to* and the verbs below.

• be • borrow • build • ~~speak~~ • swim • take

1 I *'d like to speak* Japanese.
2 He ________ some money.
3 We ________ a lot of photos.
4 You ________ your own house.
5 She ________ in the lake.
6 I ________ an actor when I'm older.

2 Complete the sentences with one word.

1 I *'d* ________ love to go horseback riding.
2 ________ you like to be a dancer?
3 We ________ love to visit you in the US.
4 They'd like ________ watch your video.
5 ________ he like to come with us?

3 Cross out the six incorrect words and write the correct statements and questions below.

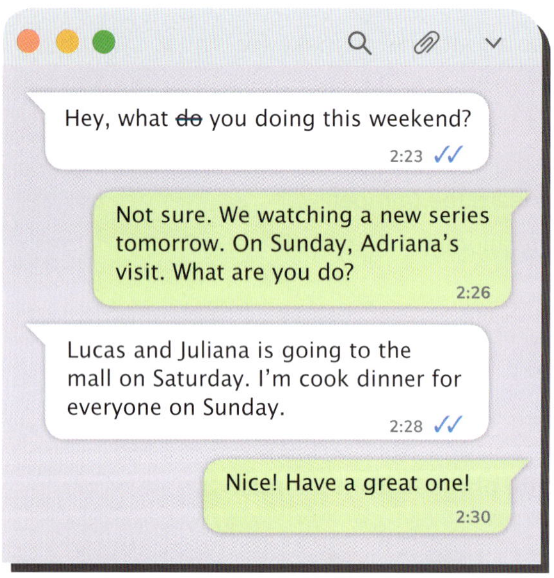

1 *Hey, what are you doing this weekend?*
2 ________
3 ________
4 ________
5 ________
6 ________

4 Write statements and questions with the prompts using the present progressive.

1 Luis / have a sleepover / tomorrow night
Luis is having a sleepover tomorrow night.
2 Lara / go to the concert / on Saturday?
____
3 Juliana and Ana / play in their band / on the weekend
____
4 I / throw a party for my best friend / next Saturday
____
5 you / do anything / tonight, Marcos?
____
6 we / eat out / this evening
____

READING

1 Look at the text and check (✓) the correct answers.

1 Why does Francisco email his aunt?
- ◯ to arrange a time to talk with her
- ◯ to tell her how he spent his birthday money
- ◯ to explain why he can't talk with her this weekend

2 What's he doing on Saturday?
- ◯ shopping
- ◯ shopping and eating out
- ◯ eating out

4: 35 p.m.

Francisco
to Camila Martinez

March 09

Hi Aunt Camila,

Sorry I didn't reply to your message yesterday. I was at my friend João's house – we were having a sleepover. It was a lot of fun. We had the best pizza and then watched gaming videos until one o'clock. I was so tired then!!!

I'd like to thank you for the money you sent for my birthday! It was very kind of you. I had a great birthday party with a lot of presents and cake. In the evening, I went to a concert with three of my best friends. It was awesome!

Mom and I would love to have a video chat with you this weekend. Sunday is probably best for us – we're doing things all day Saturday. Mom and I are going shopping in the morning. (I need some more sneakers. My feet are so big now.) After that, we're meeting Dad and Marcela for lunch at my favorite café, and in the afternoon, I'm seeing my friend David. Oh, I just remembered, we're going out in the evening, too, to celebrate Dad's birthday. It's going to be a busy day!

How are you doing? Do you have plans for the weekend? Let's speak on Sunday. Tell me what time is good for you.

Love,

Francisco

2 Read the text and check (✓) the word/phrase that completes each sentence.

1 On his birthday, Francisco ...
◯ had a sleepover. ◯ went shopping. ◯ went to a concert.

2 They can speak to Camila ...
◯ this afternoon. ◯ on Sunday. ◯ on Saturday.

3 Lunch tomorrow is with ...
◯ David. ◯ Dad and Marcela. ◯ Mom, Dad, and Marcela.

3 Answers the questions.

1 Where was Francisco yesterday?
He was at his friend João's house.

2 What did he eat at his friend's house?
....

3 Who went to a concert with him?
....

4 What's he doing on Saturday morning?
....

5 Where are they having lunch?
....

8 ONE WORLD

LANGUAGE REFERENCE

Defining Relative Clauses *who* and *that*

Relative Pronouns	Uses	Examples
who	for people	The woman **who** donated these clothes is my teacher. That's the boy **who** spoke at the ceremony.
that	for people, animals, and things	Do you remember the girl **that** swam in the competition? This is the book **that** I bought at the book fair. Is this the dog **that** your brother found on the street?

Defining relative clauses help us give essential details about something or someone.

Non-Defining Relative Clauses with *who* and *which*

who	for people	Pedro, **who** is from Panama, speaks Portuguese. Mr. Gilberto, **who** teaches math, is my new tutor.
which	for animals and things	Gorillas, **which** live in Africa, are the largest primates. *Moby Dick*, **which** is also a great book, is on TV tonight.

Non-defining relative clauses give extra information about something or someone familiar to us. We use commas to separate the non-defining relative clause. We use *who* and *which* to start these clauses, but not *that*.

Immigration

border
feel at home
immigrant
live abroad
passport
permanent resident
reside
visa

Words with Prefixes

disagree
dislike
impatient
impossible
unhappy
unkind

VOCABULARY

1 **Find eight immigration words.**

am~~immigrants~~rupermanentresidentsewresideilvisasquoborderalfeelathomehapassportsiyliveabroad

1 immigrants
2 ____________
3 ____________
4 ____________
5 ____________
6 ____________
7 ____________
8 ____________

2 **Complete the sentences with the words/phrases below.**

- border
- feel at home
- immigrant
- live abroad
- reside
- ~~visa~~

1 You need a visa to stay in the country for more than six weeks.
2 My grandfather was an ____________. He came from Portugal.
3 Our new neighbors like living in this country. I think they ____________ here.
4 I'd like to ____________ when I'm older – in the US or maybe Canada.
5 With this visa, you can stay in the country but not ____________ there.
6 We showed our passports at the ____________.

3 **Add the prefixes *dis–*, *im–*, or *un–* to make the opposite of the words in bold.**

1 I really dis **like** him.
2 Don't be so ________ **patient**!
3 I'm sorry, I ________ **agree** with you about that.
4 Some of the exercises were ________ **possible**!
5 Lara looked very ________ **happy**.
6 Gabriel said something very ________ **kind** about her.

4 **Match 1–6 with a–f.**

1 I never want to go camping. b
2 He doesn't like waiting for things. ____
3 I think he's a really good actor. ____
4 She says her daughter, only six months old, can walk. ____
5 How was Harry? ____
6 Why did you tell him he was lazy? ____

a That's impossible.
b I really dislike it.
c I thought he looked unhappy.
d That was very unkind!
e Well, I disagree with you about that.
f He's really impatient.

GRAMMAR

1 Complete the sentences with *who* or *that*.

1 This is the app ___that___ helps you translate words into English.
2 Karina's the woman __________ works in the café.
3 Where are the chocolates __________ were on the table?
4 Is that the vlogger __________ makes beauty videos?
5 She's the artist __________ paints those small pictures of birds.
6 Are you coming to the festival __________ takes place in September?

2 Circle the correct options.

1 I need to find a bag *who* / *that* is light.
2 The book *that* / *who* is on the table is my sister's book.
3 The girl *what* / *who* lives near Juan was at the party yesterday.
4 I loved the shirt *who* / *that* has big flowers.
5 The new students *who* / *what* go to our art class are really nice.
6 I love music *that* / *who* makes me relax.

3 Write one sentence with a non-defining relative clause using the two sentences and *who* or *which*.

1 Adam plays basketball. He is in my chemistry class.
Adam, who is in my chemistry class, plays basketball.
2 J. K. Rowling wrote the Harry Potter series. It is one of my favorite series.
____
3 Last year, I met Jennifer. She is a guitar player.
____
4 António do Carmo uses mainly vegetables in his recipes. He is a talented chef.
____
5 Mario loves to play Pokémon GO. It was a popular video game in 2016.
____
6 My cat Renoir enjoys playing with my sneakers. They're expensive.
____

4 Cross out the five incorrect words in the conversation and write the correct words below.

A So who's coming to the party tonight?
B Marcos and Chloe are coming. Also Aline. Aline is the girl ~~which~~ was at Juliana's house.
A Ah … the girl with the cake who was delicious?
B No, Laura was the girl that brought the cake. Aline's the girl which came from Australia last week.
A Ah, yes. You mean the girl which is pretty tall, right?
B Yes, that's her. Oh, by the way, I need to take some music to the party.
A What are you going to take?
B I'm not sure. I want some music who makes everybody dance.

1 ___who / that___ 3 __________ 5 __________
2 __________ 4 __________

READING

1 Look at the text and check (✓) the correct answers.

1 What tells you that it's an interview?
◯ a picture of a person ◯ short questions and longer answers

2 What is the objective of the interview?
◯ to compare Rakesh Kumar's country of origin and the US.
◯ to learn about Rakesh Kumar's first experiences in the US.

Focus on Immigration

As part of Grade 9's "Focus on Immigration" project, Ajay Kumar asks his grandpa, Rakesh Kumar, about his experiences as an immigrant in the 1970s.

When did you come to the US, Grandpa?

I arrived in 1975. I got off the airplane with my passport, a visa, and $300.

Didn't you bring any suitcases?

Well, I brought one small bag that belonged to my mother. But that was all.

So, you were just 21 in a completely new country. You didn't know anyone there. How did you feel? Were you unhappy?

No, I don't think I was. I mean, I was anxious, of course, but I was also very excited. It was an opportunity for me. I wanted to make a better life for myself.

But was everything different for you?

Well, some things were different, but not everything. For example, I came from a city that was crowded and noisy, and I arrived in a very populated, loud city! Anyway, I got a job after two weeks, and I found somewhere to live. I didn't have much money for several years, but I was OK. People were good to me and helped me. Very soon I felt at home. I mean, I didn't meet anyone that was really unkind. People were very nice to me.

You're always so positive, Grandpa!

2 Read the text and write *T* (true) or *F* (false) next to the statements.

1 Rakesh didn't bring any bags to the US. F
2 He already had some friends in the US when he arrived there. ....
3 He felt anxious when he arrived in the US. ....
4 He came from a place that had a lot of people. ....
5 He was poor for a short time. ....
6 He didn't feel happy or confident in the new city for many years. ....

3 Answers the questions.

1 What two documents did Rakesh bring to the US?
He brought his passport and a visa.

2 How much money did he bring?
....

3 What did he want to do in the US?
....

4 How does he describe the city where he was living in the US?
....

5 How long did it take him to find a job?
....

Thanks and Acknowledgements

We would like to thank the following people for their invaluable contribution to the series:

Ruth Atkinson, Justine Gesell, Tom Hadland, S. Bastian Harris, Cara Norris, Maria Toth, Joep van der Werff, Kate Woodford and Liz Walter.

The authors and editors would like to thank all the teachers who have contributed to the development of the course:

Geysla Lopes de Alencar, Priscila Araújo, David Williams Mocock de Araújo, Leticia da Silva Azevedo, Francisco Evangelista Ferreira Batista, Luiz Fernando Carmo, Thiago Silva Campos, Cintia Castilho, Mônica Egydio, Érica Fernandes, Viviane Azevêdo de Freitas, Marco Giovanni, Rodolfo de Aro da Rocha Keizer, Vanessa Leroy, Bruno Fernandes de Lima, Allana Tavares Maciel, Jonadab Mansur, Rogério dos Santos Melo, Carlos Ubiratã Gois de Menezes, Aryanne Moreira, Joelba Geane da Silva, Vanessa Silva Pereira, Daniela Costa Pinheiro, Isa de França Vasconcelos, Eliana Perrucci Vergani, Geraldo Vieira, Whebston Mozart.

The authors and publishers acknowledge the following sources of copyright material and are grateful for the permissions granted. While every effort has been made, it has not always been possible to identify the sources of all the material used, or to trace all copyright holders. If any omissions are brought to our notice, we will be happy to include the appropriate acknowledgements on reprinting and in the next update to the digital edition, as applicable.

Keys: EM = End Matter, P = Projects, R = Review, U = Unit, W = Welcome,

Student's Book

Text

U3: Text about 'Niam Jain'. Reproduced with kind permission; **P2:** Table based on 'Migration, Australia: Table 1.5 Australia's population by country of birth - 2018(a)' by Australian Bureau of Statistics, https://www.abs.gov.au/statistics/people/population/migration-australia/2017-18. Copyright © 2018 Commonwealth of Australia, CC BY 4.0 licence; Graph based on 'Migration, Australia: Graph 1.3 Overseas-born-top 10 countries of birth- Australia-2009, 2014 and 2019' by Australian Bureau of Statistics, https://www.abs.gov.au/statistics/people/population/migration-australia/latest-release. Copyright © 2019 Commonwealth of Australia, CC BY 4.0 licence.

Photography

The following images are sourced from Getty Images.

UW: mathisworks/DigitalVision Vectors; Sibani Das/iStock; supriadi supriadi/iStock; LysenkoAlexander/iStock; Fidan Babayeva/iStock; Sumberyotro/iStock; priyanka gupta/iStock; AVIcons; Lyudmila_K/Istock; Bryan Rodrguez/EyeEm; DigiPub/Moment; fcafotodigital/E+; Foodcollection; rambo182/DigitalVision Vectors; martin-dm/E+; Cavan Images; kali9/E+; Russ Rohde/Cultura; RF Pictures/The Image Bank; da-vooda/iStock; CSA Images; Dedy Setyawan/iStock; mustafahacalaki/DigitalVision Vectors; LueratSatichob/DigitalVision Vectors; -VICTOR-/DigitalVision Vectors; appleuzr/DigitalVision Vectors; DivVector/DigitalVision Vectors; ilyaliren/iStock; kiszon pascal/Moment; Jorg Greuel/Stone; Michael Blann/DigitalVision; Jon Hicks/Stone; mbbirdy/E+; fotoVoyager/iStock Unreleased; **U1:** graphixel/E+; Luka Isakadze/EyeEm; Narinder Nanu/AFP; Nisian Hughes/Stone; Toshi Sasaki/Photographer's Choice; skynesher/E+; Newton Daly/DigitalVision; Jesper Guldbrand/EyeEm; HSU SHIH-CHEN/Moment; PeopleImages/E+; Sam Yeh/AFP; Prostock-Studio/iStock; Glow Images; Konstantin Kolosov/500Px Plus; simon2579/DigitalVision Vectors; wildestanimal/Moment; Charriau Pierre/The Image Bank; Stefano Mazzola/Awakening/Getty Images Entertainment; Carl Court/Getty Images News; Klaus Vedfelt/DigitalVision; picture alliance; Symphonie Ltd/Cultura; Hans-Peter Merten/Photodisc; simonkr/E+; Attasit Singkaew/EyeEm; Education Images/Universal Images Group; Gonzalo Azumendi/Stone; Jose Jordan/AFP; Jose Luis Pelaez Inc/DigitalVision; benzoix/iStock; SteveStone/iStock; Benoist SEBIRE/Moment; kali9/E+; **U2:** Anupong Sakoolchai/Moment; Smart/iStock; Pacharada17/iStock; kolotuschenko/iStock; calvindexter/DigitalVision Vectors; South_agency/DigitalVision Vectors; Mike Korostelev/Moment; Afriandi/Moment Open; tdub_video/E+; JeffGoulden/E+; Spacewalk/iStock; Ratnakorn Piyasirisorost/Moment; Pete Rowbottom/Moment; Robert Kneschke/EyeEm; Franz Aberham/The Image Bank; apomares/E+; Punnawit Suwuttananun/Moment; Grant Faint/DigitalVision; Image Source/DigitalVision; Ig0rZh/iStock; Patrick Orton; Gillian Henry/Moment; Science Photo Library - NASA/Brand X Pictures; Ashley Cooper/The Image Bank Unreleased; Albert Klein/Oxford Scientific; kiszon pascal/Moment; Argijale/Moment; Michael Runkel; Westend61; Francesco Vaninetti Photo/Moment; **R1 and 2:** Viaframe/Stone; Tibor Bognar/The Image Bank Unreleased; Susie Adams/Moment; LatinContent/LatinContent WO; Eric Lafforgue/Art in All of Us/Corbis News; Westend61; **U3:** beastfromeast/DigitalVision Vectors; Albert Klein/Oxford Scientific; David Young-Wolff/The Image Bank; Richard Drury/Stone; SolStock/Moment; Cavan Images; ViewStock; asbe/E+; Aleksandras Zvirzdinas/500px; Poras Chaudhary/The Image Bank; jacoblund/iStock; Stockbyte; FatCamera/E+; Guido Mieth/Moment; Jupiterimages/Polka Dot; vgajic/E+; Wladimir Bulgar/Science Photo Library; Timmary/iStock; Jacqui Hurst/Corbis NX; David Malan/Stone; John M Lund Photography Inc/Stone; Nicola Tree/Stone; Mirko Vitali/EyeEm; Hill Street Studios/DigitalVision; David Silverman/Getty Images News; fstop123/E+; Alys Tomlinson/DigitalVision; domoyega/E+; dolgachov/iStock; mediaphotos/iStock; Anadolu Agency/Getty Images News; Tom Merton/OJO Images; **U4:** Westend61; Oli_Trolly/iStock; Narat Kongsawat/EyeEm; GCShutter/E+; SDI Productions/E+; Eric Audras/ONOKY; sabelskaya/iStock; William Whitehurst/The Image Bank; allanswart/iStock; MOAimage/Moment; NurPhoto; Pichai Pipatkuldilok/EyeEm; Animaflora/iStock; ankmsn/iStock; MirageC/Moment; mediaphotos/iStock; ClaudioVentrella/iStock; MoMo Productions/DigitalVision; pioneer111/iStock; **R3 and 4:** shekaka/iStock; DreamPictures/The Image Bank; John M Lund Photography Inc/DigitalVision; Finnbarr Webster/Getty Images News; czarny_bez/iStock; Ljupco/iStock; Aldo Murillo/iStock; Marcus Lindstrom/E+; Barcin/iStock; Jonelle Weaver/Photolibrary; laymul/iStock; dlerick/iStock; Image Source; Peter Dazeley/The Image Bank; **U5:** Photographer is my life/Moment; Alex Segre/Moment; Manuel Breva Colmeiro/Moment; Jose Luis Pelaez Inc/DigitalVision; PeopleImages/E+; Epoxydude; Tom and Steve/Moment; MStudioImages/E+; John M Lund Photography Inc/DigitalVision; Preto_perola/iStock; Marta Ortiz/iStock; Marina Borovskaya/iStock; Pollyana Ventura/E+; Jose Luis Pelaez/Photodisc; Colorblind Images LLC/DigitalVision; Maskot/DigitalVision; cometary/iStock; Andersen Ross/Stockbyte; Brian Mitchell/Corbis Documentary; Huntstock; KeithBishop/DigitalVision Vectors; Matthias Tunger/Photodisc; **U6:** martin-dm/E+; Jack Thomas/Getty Images Sport; Michael Ochs Archives; Print Collector/Hulton Archive; Vladi333/iStock; Kurt Krieger - Corbis/Corbis Entertainment; FierceAbin/E+; Ferdaus Shamim/WireImage; Gustavo Caballero/Getty Images Entertainment; Hagen Hopkins/Getty Images News; ZU_09/DigitalVision Vectors; PCH-Vector/iStock; Esra Sen Kula/DigitalVision Vectors; lushik/DigitalVision Vectors; PeterSnow/iStock; Stock Ninja Studio/iStock; ilyast/DigitalVision Vectors; Turac Novruzova/iStock; Designer/DigitalVision Vectors; the8monkey/iStock; Lawrence Manning/Corbis; guy-ozenne/iStock; Isabel Pavia/Moment; Prostock-Studio/iStock; Phill Thornton/iStock; Francesco Milanese/iStock; artpartner-images/The Image Bank; leezsnow/E+; Gerasimov174/iStock; VacharapongW/iStock; sqback/iStock; Yuliia Moisieieva/iStock; Volodymyr Kotoshchuk/iStock; stockerteam/iStock; AFP Contributor; herraez/iStock; Maskot; Barney Britton/Redferns; Robin Marchant/Getty Images Entertainment; Thana Prasongsin/Moment; sukanya sitthikongsak/Moment; **R5 and 6:** Yasser Chalid/Moment; Dimitri Otis/Stone; Sasha_Suzi/iStock; Prostock-Studio/iStock; Nick David/Stone; samopinny/iStock; **U7:** SDI Productions/E+; JohnnyGreig/E+; Klaus Vedfelt/DigitalVision; Lydie Gigerichova; Emilija Manevska/Moment; Brosa/E+; Witthaya Prasongsin/Moment; Niedring/Drentwett/Alloy; Compassionate Eye Foundation/Martin Barraud/Stone; Daisy-Daisy/iStock; Sudowoodo/iStock; bortonia/DigitalVision Vectors; davidcreacion/iStock; AaronAmat/iStock; denisgorelkin/iStock; 4zevar/iStock; Turqay Melikli/iStock; simonkr/E+; skynesher/E+; vgajic/E+; Photodisc; Lisa-Blue/E+; franckreporter/E+; fstop123/E+; S-S-S/iStock; Maksym Rudoi/iStock; Elena Brovko/iStock; Ville Heikkinen/iStock; Stefan Dinse/EyeEm; Ismael Juan Salcedo/EyeEm; five_star_photography/iStock; David Clapp/Stone; Hill Street Studios/DigitalVision; **U8:** Digital Vision./Photodisc; CursedSenses/iStock; Tim Hall/Cultura; FG Trade/E+; Michael Dunning/The Image Bank; Pekic/E+; xavierarnau/E+; Sally Anscombe/DigitalVision; Image Source/DigitalVision; Pongnathee Kluaythong/EyeEm; Morsa Images/DigitalVision; Aleksandr Zubkov/Moment; Damien Meyer/AFP; SDI Productions/E+; Rob Lewine; Cattleya Tothanarungroj/EyeEm; Natasha Breen/Moment;/DigitalVision; **R7 and 8:** Carol Yepes/Moment; Isabel Pavia/Moment; Jasmin Merdan/Moment; Corey Jenkins/Image Source; Justin Paget/DigitalVision; tacojim/E+; Westend61; anyaivanova/iStock; EM: Masahiro Hayata/Moment; MIXA; Alfredo Estrella/AFP; Eric PHAN-KIM/Moment; De Agostini/Archivio J. Lange/De Agostini Picture Library; DEA/W. BUSS/De Agostini; David Molina/500px/500Px Plus; Trevor Williams/Stone; Nicholas Hylton/EyeEm; Elva Etienne/Moment; BJI/Blue Jean Images; Image Source/DigitalVision; pixelfit/E+; zakokor/iStock; Holloway/Stone; dmbaker/iStock; Robert Recker/The Image Bank; GeorgePeters/E+; lenanet/iStock; Maskot; PeopleImages/E+; Westend61; goglik83/iStock; Brownie Harris/The Image Bank; PM Images/DigitalVision; John Giustina/The Image Bank; Xphi Chnm Phechr Nùn/EyeEm; Kathleen Finlay/Image Source; Morsa Images/DigitalVision; yongyuan/E+; SDI Productions/E+; Jasmin Merdan/Moment; P1: Thien Woei Jiing/iStock Editorial; Muslianshah Masrie/Photodisc. Klaus Vedfelt/DigitalVision; Yuji Kotani/DigitalVision; R7 and 8: